# Heathrow

At ten years old, George Hayter was se
from his home. Other boys were from fu
plantations in Africa, in commerce in In ﹍ ﹍ ﹍ the forces in
Australia. Dormitory conversations about school holidays always
seemed to be about Comets to Nairobi, or 707s to Beirut. Inevitably these
extravagant travelogues engendered feelings of inferiority in the boy
whose parents only lived down the road. At the heart of these stories was
London Airport – Heathrow – and young George developed a curiosity
about the place.

After he left school he got to know Heathrow and read all he could about
it. He delved into old maps, photographs and newspapers. He inter-
viewed the men who ran the airport in its early years. He unearthed
documents which revealed political intrigue in getting the airport built,
and he went further back, and traced some of the former residents of the
country village of Heathrow.

In addition to his fascination for Heathrow Airport, George loves flying,
specially at the controls of a Chipmunk or Cherokee. He has travelled
widely on five continents. He works for BBC TV as a computer graphics
operator, and lives in West London.

George Hayter

# Heathrow

maps by Ken Smith

**Pan Books London**
Sydney and Auckland

First published 1989 by Pan Books Ltd,
Cavaye Place, London SW10 9PG

9 8 7 6 5 4 3 2 1

© George Hayter 1989

ISBN 0 330 30897 1

Photoset by Parker Typesetting Service, Leicester

Printed and bound in Great Britain by
Hazell Watson & Viney Limited,
Member of the BPCC Limited,
Aylesbury, Bucks, England

To my father

Where the place?
                    Upon the heath.

*Macbeth Act 1 Scene 1*

# Contents

# List of illustrations

**Photographs**

The Great West Aerodrome in 1935. (British Airports Authority)

Formalities to mark the first passenger-carrying flight from Heathrow, 1 January 1946. (BBC Hulton Picture Library)

The terminal area at Heathrow, 1946. (British Airports Authority)

The original RAF control tower in 1952 (P. Clifton)

The passenger tunnel under construction, about 1952. (Taylor Woodrow)

Terminal 3 when it was first opened in 1961. (Taylor Woodrow)

The Central Area, around 1964. (Taylor Woodrow)

The airport emergency services deal with the burning 707. (British Airports Authority)

Heathrow in the 1970s. (British Airports Authority)

Cain's Lane in 1987. (The author)

Terminal 4. (British Airports Authority)

**Maps and diagrams**

## Acknowledgements

I'm indebted to the trees who gave in order that this book might be produced. Their sacrifice was the ultimate one; others were almost as generous.

I spent many hours poring over maps and photographs spread out on the dining table of Alastair Macrae, whose familiarity with the airport was invaluable. Mr Macrae patiently answered lists of questions, and he later eliminated numerous technical errors when he was kind enough to read one of the final drafts.

I owe much to Lord Balfour of Inchrye. Despite modest protestations of 'It's all so long ago', Lord Balfour recalled as much as any individual I approached.

Air Vice-Marshal Donald Bennett sacrificed an all too rare sunny afternoon in his magnificent garden to stay indoors speaking into my tape recorder, giving me more than two hours of detailed answers.

Sir Peter Masefield graciously found time to help me, vividly bringing the Fairey aerodrome to life, and speaking frankly about the BAA.

Sir Nigel Foulkes also interrupted a busy schedule to delve into the past.

I'm grateful to Group Captain Jimmy Jeffs for his enthusiastic recollections.

Ray Berry of Heathrow Airport Limited spent many hours checking an early draft, pencilling lengthy notes in the margin. His staff in Public Relations were also helpful and encouraging.

I'm extremely grateful to Philip Sherwood of Hayes and Harlington Local History Society. Mr Sherwood has a detailed knowledge of the Heathrow area, and he readily shared with me all that he knew.

A. H. Cox, another leading local historian, also explained much about Heathrow before the airport.

I was fortunate to find many others who also knew a great deal about Heathrow village. Some live close to the airport, while others have moved elsewhere in the Home Counties. I would like to thank particularly H. J. Philp, G. A. Philp and Miss Falconer.

David Kerridge was kind enough to send me the writings of David Wild, who used to run a market garden where Terminal 2 stands today.

R. A. R. Wilson of Aviation Historical Services gave me a number of useful tips, and provided access to the British Airways archives at the RAF Museum, Hendon.

Sue Baker at Taylor Woodrow found pictures which spoke volumes about the construction of the Central Area. Other useful sources were the CAA Library, CAA Press Office, and the British Library. The Royal Aeronautical Society helped with the garden parties. Documents in the Public Record Office at Kew shed light on events in government during the Second World War. I'm grateful to many helpful souls at the BAA's Masefield House, particularly Bob Cook and Susan Carter.

Thanks to Hounslow library for letting me rummage through their old maps, photographs and back issues of local papers. I got a lot of help, too, from the local history section at Uxbridge library, under the direction of Jane Wood.

Annie Jackson, of Pan Books, skilfully juggled the paragraphs and tactfully showed me where the penultimate draft was unclear or confusing.

My wife gave unique encouragement, specially when I hit a low in late '87. Thanks for the card, Jan.

# Chronology

| | |
|---|---|
| Nov 1937 | Heston purchased by the Air Ministry for use as the main London airport |
| 30 Sept 1938 | Neville Chamberlain returns to Heston with a promise of peace from Hitler |
| 4 Aug 1939 | Air Ministry (Heston and Kenley Aerodromes Extension) Act |
| Feb 1943 | Harold Balfour asks Sir Arthur Street to examine Heathrow as a possible airport site |
| Oct 1943 | Sir Archibald Sinclair puts the Heathrow proposal before Cabinet |
| 10 Nov 1943 | First Cabinet Committee meeting to consider building a great airport at Heathrow |
| 27 Jan 1944 | Second and last of the Cabinet Committee meetings concludes that a very large airport should be built at Heathrow |
| March 1944 | General Critchley announces his discovery of an unnamed site, which he declares suitable for a great airport |
| 12 June 1944 | *The Daily Telegraph* reports that construction has begun |
| 8 Oct 1944 | Lord Swinton appointed first Minister of Civil Aviation |
| 10 May 1945 | Ministry meeting: Short term policy for London airports |
| 4 Aug 1945 | Lord Winster becomes Minister of Civil Aviation |
| 13 Aug 1945 | Another Ministry meeting considers London's airports |
| Sept 1945 | Layout Panel appointed |
| Oct 1945 | Transport Command take over Heathrow |
| 20 Oct 1945 | Bennett asks for permission to start services from Heathrow |
| 24 Oct 1945 | First scheduled transatlantic passenger flight by land plane |
| 6 Dec 1945 | BSAA land at Heathrow for the first time |
| 1 Jan 1946 | Heathrow passes to Ministry of Civil Aviation |
| 1 Jan 1946 | First scheduled departure, by BSAA |
| 13 March 1946 | House of Lords announcement of closure of Heston |
| 25 March 1946 | Lord Winster announces the name 'London Airport' |
| 28 May 1946 | First scheduled BOAC arrival |
| 31 May 1946 | Official opening |
| 19 Sept 1946 | First triangle of runways completed |
| 30 Jan 1947 | Layout Panel report published |

| | |
|---|---|
| 25 July 1947 | Harold Wilson injured |
| 2 Mar 1948 | Sabena Dakota crashes |
| 2 June 1949 | First Stratocruiser lands |
| 16 April 1950 | First scheduled BEA departure |
| 23 Oct 1950 | Taylor Woodrow start work on the passenger tunnel |
| 31 Oct 1950 | BEA Viking crash |
| 1 Feb 1952 | Princess Elizabeth and Prince Philip seen off by George VI |
| 7 Feb 1952 | Elizabeth returns as Queen |
| 2 May 1952 | World's first scheduled jet departure |
| Dec 1952 | Commons announcement that there will be no airport development north of the Bath Road |
| 2 May 1953 | First Comet crash, near Calcutta |
| 7 Oct 1953 | Passenger tunnel inaugurated |
| 1954 | End of civil aviation facilities at Northolt |
| 10 Jan 1954 | Second Comet crash, off Elba |
| 8 Apr 1954 | Third Comet disaster, off Naples |
| 13 June 1954 | Last Garden Party |
| 15 June 1954 | Alcock and Brown statue unveiled |
| 16 Jan 1955 | BEA Viscount crash |
| 17 Apr 1955 | Central Area comes partly into use |
| 16 Dec 1955 | The Queen officially opens the Central Area |
| 1 Oct 1956 | RAF Vulcan crash |
| 1 Aug 1957 | Millbourn Committee report |
| 4 Oct 1958 | First transatlantic scheduled jets started by BOAC |
| 16 Nov 1961 | BOAC moves into Oceanic Building |
| 28 March 1962 | Other longhaul operators move into Oceanic Building |
| 20 Aug 1963 | Opening of Heathrow's first multi-storey car park (now known as Terminal 2 Car Park) |
| 1964 | M4 motorway opens near Heathrow |
| 1965 | M4 spur to Heathrow opens |
| 2 June 1965 | Airports Authority Act |
| 27 Oct 1965 | BEA Vanguard crash |
| 1 Apr 1966 | BAA 'vesting date' |
| 19 Apr 1966 | Opening of second multi-storey car park (now known as Terminal 3 Car Park) |
| 8 Apr 1968 | BOAC 707 fire |

| | |
|---|---|
| 11 June 1968 | Arrival of Daniel Cohn-Bendit sparks demonstration |
| 3 July 1968 | BKS Ambassador crashes with horses aboard |
| 11 Oct 1968 | Chapel opens |
| 6 Nov 1968 | Terminal 1 opens to domestic traffic |
| 1 Dec 1968 | Introduction of red and green Customs channels |
| Dec 1968 | Faults found in passenger tunnel roof |
| Dec 1968 | Cargo terminal comes onstream |
| 9 Feb 1969 | At Everett, the first ever 747 takes off |
| 17 Apr 1969 | Terminal 1 inaugurated by HM The Queen |
| 7 May 1969 | Terminal 1 in full operation |
| 12 Jan 1970 | Arrival of first 747 proving flight |
| 21 Jan 1970 | Arrival of first 747 scheduled flight |
| March 1970 | CHAOS demonstration |
| 1 June 1970 | 747 complex inaugurated |
| 1 Apr 1971 | Edinburgh joins BAA |
| 1 Jan 1972 | Peter Masefield knighted. Nigel Foulkes takes over as BAA Chairman |
| 18 June 1972 | BEA Trident crash near Staines |
| 2 July 1972 | Michael Heseltine announces the setting up of British Airways |
| 1973 | Runway 27 Left is overslabbed |
| 1974 | Runway 27 Right is overslabbed |
| Spring 1974 | Maplin project abandoned by Labour |
| 29 Apr 1974 | Roy Jenkins announces the end of the BAA Constabulary |
| 4 May 1974 | Turkish Airlines DC-10 crashes near Paris |
| 4 May 1974 | British Airways VC-10 blown up |
| 19 May 1974 | Terminal 1 bomb |
| 1 Jan 1975 | Aberdeen joins the BAA |
| 7 Jan 1975 | BEA 1-11 hijack |
| 12 Jan 1975 | First shuttle service |
| 1 Apr 1975 | Glasgow joins the BAA |
| July 1975 | Hatton Cross Underground station opens |
| 21 Jan 1976 | World's first scheduled supersonic departure |
| 1 March 1977 | Norman Payne replaces Nigel Foulkes as BAA Chairman |
| 26 Sept 1977 | At Gatwick, Skytrain enters service |

16 Dec 1977    Heathrow Central Underground station opened by HM the Queen
Apr 1978    Charter flights banned from Heathrow
9 June 1978    Gatwick airlink inaugurated
Apr 1981    Eurolounge inaugurated
26 Nov 1983    Brinks-Mat robbery
22 Apr 1984    Terminal 2 bomb
June 1985    Publication of 'Airports Policy' White Paper
Oct 1985    Schockemoehle robbed
9 Jan 1986    First regular deployment of machine guns within terminal buildings
1 Apr 1986    Prince and Princess of Wales open Terminal 4
12 Apr 1986    Terminal 4 actually comes into operation
17 Apr 1986    Nezar Hindawi bomb plot foiled
1 Aug 1986    Formation of BAA plc
28 July 1987    Debut of BAA shares on the London Stock Exchange
Summer 1988    Unprecedented air traffic control delays

**1754** Heathrow consists of a row of houses facing an expanse of heath

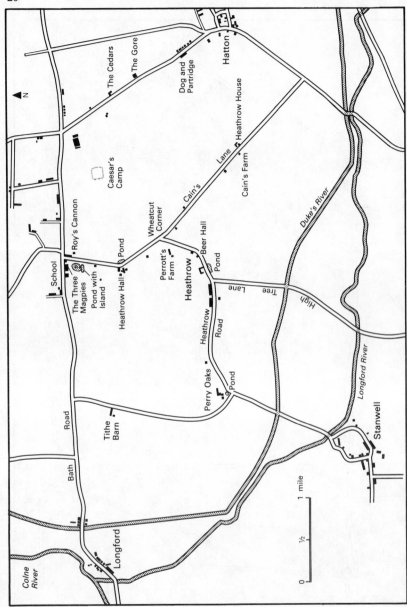

**1915** The heath has been cultivated. Numerous ponds have appeared in Heathrow. Cain's Lane and High Tree Lane are transformed from vague paths into established roads

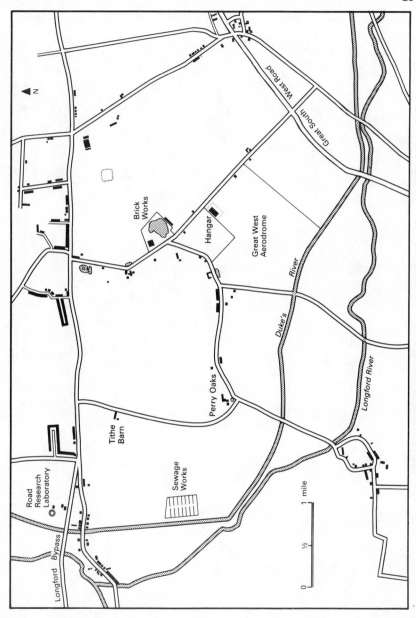

**1939** Both the brickworks and Fairey's Great West Aerodrome are in operation. Longford bypass and the Great South West Road appear for the first time. A new sewage works is on stream west of Perry Oaks

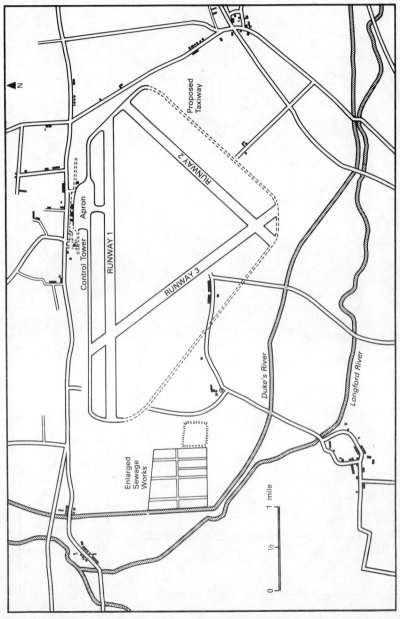

Control Tower

Apron

RUNWAY 1

RUNWAY 2

RUNWAY 3

Proposed Taxiway

Enlarged Sewage Works

Duke's River

Longford River

0    ½    1 mile

N

**1946** Most of the village is destroyed, replaced by three enormous runways laid out in the standard RAF triangular pattern. The peripheral taxiway is destined never to be completed

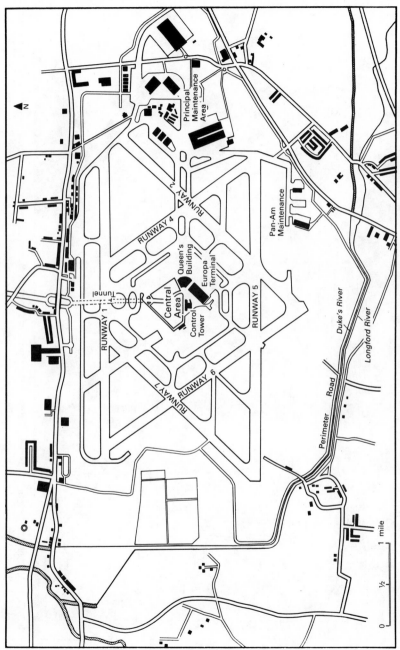

**1955** More houses, roads and trees have been wiped away, and Duke's River has been diverted to the south. The airfield has expanded, and now boasts six runways. The first three buildings are open in the Central Area. To the east, vast hangars in the new maintenance area have obliterated much of Hatton

N

Principal
Maintenance
Area

RUNWAY 2

RUNWAY 4

Queen's
Building

Europa
Terminal

Central
Area

Control
Tower

Tunnel

RUNWAY 1

Pan-Am
Maintenance

RUNWAY 5

RUNWAY 6

RUNWAY 7

Duke's River

Longford River

Perimeter Road

0    ½    1 mile

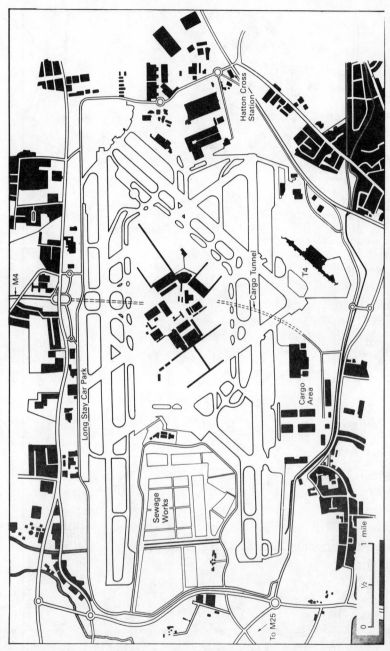

**1989** Central Area building has expanded on to three of the runways. Only three runways remain in use, two of them lengthened towards the west. On the southern perimeter there is a new area for handling cargo, and a new passenger terminal

# Arrival

Sometimes big airports get so busy that arriving aircraft have to wait before they can land. Air crew literally fly around in circles to kill time, usually above a radio beacon. One of these is at Biggin Hill airfield near Croydon. On a clear day you can see airliners patiently circling in a stack above Biggin, then gratefully peeling off to make their final approach to Heathrow.

Usually this is from the east, because in Britain the prevailing wind is from the west, and even modern airliners like to land into the wind. That way their speed relative to the ground is lower than their airspeed, allowing them to stop in a shorter, safer distance.

So our arriving aeroplane finds itself following a course into Heathrow which offers some of the most spectacular urban views in the world. Passengers with a window seat on the right of the plane see the River Thames below them, gradually narrowing as the centre of London approaches. Then the bridges start, Tower Bridge looming up like a gateway to the City. The dome of St Paul's Cathedral floats by, then the Gothic intricacy of the Houses of Parliament. The aircraft steadily loses height as it passes Buckingham Palace and Hammersmith Bridge, Kew Gardens and Osterley Park.

A radar screen in the cockpit shows the pilots any aircraft ahead, or a vague map-like image of the ground they are passing over, or they can even switch it to show passing clouds and areas of rain. But neither the captain, who sits on the left, nor his co-pilot will be relying on his radar at this point.

The course of any airliner is supervised by Air Traffic Control (ATC). The pilot is passed on from one ATC to another as he crosses the air space of different countries. Heathrow Approach has its own ATC. This dictates the speed, height and direction of planes so that they line up one behind the other to approach the runway with a safe interval between the arrival of each. That they do this without colliding is a considerable achievement of technology, clear thinking and, according to some, luck. A few slow-moving propeller-driven aircraft mixed in with the jets add further to the complexity.

As our plane passes through 2,000 feet somewhere over Richmond the undercarriage is lowered, producing an audible rumbling in the passenger cabin. On the flight deck the autopilot is adjusted to reduce the speed to about 180 m.p.h. From the backs of the wings flaps are extended to increase the wing area and keep the machine in the air at low speed. Leading edge slats extended from the fronts of the wings also have the effect of increasing lift.

At each end of Heathrow's three runways a fence-like structure topped with alternate red and white rectangles sends a radio beam down the length of the runway. The beam extends several miles beyond the far end of the runway, and is pointed slightly into the sky, at an angle of 3° above the horizontal.

Every plane fitted with the ingenious Instrument Landing System will approach the runway along this beam. If the plane should drift to the left or right, the ILS indicator on the flight deck tells the pilot which way to turn to get back on to the beam. Similarly, if the plane should drop below the 3° glide path the system tells the pilot to gain height, and if he's too high he sees he has to use throttle and flaps to lose height. In this way all the airliners approaching Heathrow fly through exactly the same slice of sky one after another on their way in. With their landing headlights shining this makes a terrific spectacle, particularly at the peak times of Friday and Sunday nights in the summer.

As our airliner slides down the glide path it is getting closer to touchdown at Heathrow. Passengers on the left may glimpse unwittingly a symptom of malaise in the society amidst which they are about to land. Riot City is a former army barracks where the police are trained to contain civil unrest. Riots have broken out in English cities in the last quarter of the century, and in 1985 a policeman was killed. So here at Hounslow, police cadets act as rioters, but throw harmless tennis balls instead of bricks. The bobbies learn to use riot shields to protect themselves from missiles, including Molotov cocktails. Battle scenes are acted out in mock streets where the façades have no buildings behind them, and from the air many passengers mistake Riot City for a movie set.

Next the plane passes Hounslow Heath, the historic site of an earlier and much smaller London airport. The Brinks-Mat warehouse, scene of Britain's biggest ever robbery, disappears under the starboard wing. Nine seconds later the aircraft is over Hatton Green, a housing estate built for the former residents of Hatton Road, whose homes were demolished to make way for the airport. Agile passengers may glimpse the Green Man pub, built in 1627 and reputedly once the haunt of highwaymen, as that too flashes by.

By now the flight crew can see the VASI lights on either side of the runway. These Visual Approach Slope Indicators tell them whether they are at the right height, as an optical confirmation of the ILS. If the plane is approaching too low, both VASI lights show red, too high and they both show white. If the approach is just right, the further VASI shows red and the nearer is white.

By now the airliner is over the approach lights. Between two of the pylons that support these lights is the last house before the airfield perimeter. For the occupants, the noise is deafening, and

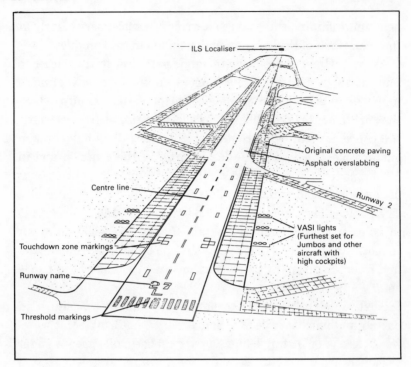

Runway 27 Left

after the plane has passed over the chimney they are often left with a strong swirling wind known as the vortex.

Down to perhaps 140 m.p.h. by now, the jet seems to glide over the A30, on over the perimeter fence, and, just a few feet above the ground, over the 'zebra crossing' markings at the start or threshold of the runway. Helped by the VASI lights, the pilot will be aiming to land in the touchdown zone, some way along from the threshold and marked by white lines in the shape of brackets. If there is a strong cross-wind the aircraft will inevitably be approaching slightly crab-like, and it has to be 'kicked straight' with the rudder pedals just before touchdown. If this is done too soon the plane will be carried sideways by the wind and will miss the runway.

In the last seconds the co-pilot calls out the altitude in feet: 'one hundred . . . fifty . . . thirty'. To make a smooth landing the pilot has to slow the rate of descent just before contact with the asphalt. This is the art of 'flaring'. Once the weight is on the tyres, 'lift dumpers' are immediately hinged out of the upper surfaces of the wing to cause turbulence, stopping the wings acting like wings, and keeping the speeding plane safely glued to the ground.

Speed is now rapidly reduced by putting the engines into reverse thrust. The mechanics vary with different engines, but all involve deflecting the exhaust gases from the turbine or fan so that they shoot out forwards, in the same direction as the aircraft is moving. Deceleration is assisted by the brakes which are fitted to all wheels, and which the pilots apply with toe pedals. Below 80 m.p.h. the rudder becomes ineffective and direction is controlled by a steering wheel connected to the nose wheel.

The progress of our aeroplane is now supervised by one of the Runway Controllers perched in the Ground Control Room at the top of the Control Tower. He tells the pilots which of the many turnings from the runway they should use. Once on the maze of taxiways, another young man or woman in Ground Control guides them through the one-way traffic system of taxiways around the Central Area, to get them to their alloted stand. The instructions are always in simple, unambiguous English. 'Turn left', 'turn right' or 'give way to the Air India 747 on your right'.

At peak times a plane arrives at Heathrow about every ninety seconds. With its 35 million passengers a year, this is the fifth busiest airport in the world, behind Chicago O'Hare (60 million), Atlanta (48), Los Angeles (45) and Dallas (41). But more than 80 per cent of Heathrow's passengers are travelling to or from a foreign country. That's twenty-nine million passengers every year, all on international flights, easily the world's highest total, giving Heathrow the distinction of being the world's most international airport. the number of foreign airlines that use Heathrow is also higher than for anywhere else, and you can fly to more international destinations from Heathrow than from any other airport.

The busy US fields may have the most passengers, but they've little of the romantic quality of a Heathrow. Though big, they're bland. A third of a million aeroplanes land at Chicago in a year, but most are American airlines bringing American businessmen from other American cities. By contrast the stands at Heathrow are graced by exotic liveries from throughout the globe. The terminals bring together Africans and Asians, Europeans and Antipodeans. Caribbean patter and the dialects of India resound amongst fezzes and turbans, keffiyehs and yashmaks.

This is the most international place on earth, the crossroads of the globe.

# 1
# Countryside

Heathrow began to take shape when part of the chalk foundations of south-east England collapsed like a mis-timed soufflé twenty-five million years ago and the resulting depression became the Thames valley. A succession of advances and retreats by the sea and the meanderings of the Thames left a flat deposit of gravel here. This extraordinary flatness was to be just what was needed by aviators five million years later.

In the meantime other qualities of this place were discovered by an earlier people. About the time that Stonehenge was being heaved together, a neolithic tribe settled here, probably because the gravel foundations offer good drainage, a prized feature in marshy ancient Britain. The River Colne would also have been a useful amenity 4,000 years ago. Close by its waters the tribe made a clearing in the damp forest which then covered most of these islands, and they seem to have settled down to an agricultural way of life.

The next thing archaeologists can tell us about Heathrow is that there was another settlement, this one a couple of miles away from the Colne, and about 2,000 years later. Here Celts made themselves a fortified 450-foot rectangular enclosure and lived within its earthen banks in eleven round wooden huts of varying sizes and built at different times. A larger rectangular building had a shallow roof and may have looked like a distant timber copy of a Greek temple.

There is no evidence that the Romans settled at Heathrow, but they did build one of their celebrated straight military roads a mile to the south of what is now the airport. This London to Staines thoroughfare made upon the area a permanent impact which is still evident today.

Further north a village pops up for the first time in the Domesday Book. This settlement by the Colne still stands today. Picturesque Harmondsworth still has its church on the original site, and a cavernous fifteenth-century tithe barn, supported by great oak beams and still in agricultural use.

In the thirteenth century Henry III cleared the forest on both sides of the Roman road, all the way from Staines to Brentford. This impressive undertaking created Hounslow Heath. Three centuries later the River Colne was partly diverted, to introduce two rivers for the first time across the future airport site. Duke of Northumberland's River was probably created to boost the power of Isleworth Water Mill on the River Crane. Longford River – sometimes called Cardinal's River – was dreamed up to supplement the decorative pools of the new palace at Hampton Court.

Heathrow has been known by a variety of names over the years. In the fifteenth century it was Hetherewe, in the sixteenth century Hetherow or Hitherowe, and in the seventeenth century Hedrowe. The earliest map which shows the place is Rocque's Middlesex map of 1754. It shows a string of houses spread out along the road marking the western boundary of the heath. This road became Heathrow Road. Heathrow never did amount to much more than a procession of houses along this lane, beginning to spread in the last years down Cain's Lane and High Tree Lane as well. There was never the compactness or the central focus, such as a church, needed to make Heathrow a true village. Yet village we must call it because with a population of several hundred it grew into more than a hamlet.

The old Roman road became the main highway from London to

the south-west of England, used by coaches and horses. The original pavement fell into disrepair and there were treacherous pot-holes to slow down travel and make it uncomfortable and dirty. Carriage wheels regularly had to be dug out of the mud. Where the road crossed the bleak emptiness of Hounslow Heath it had by the seventeenth century become an infamous haunt of ruthless highwaymen. Even Dick Turpin is alleged to have operated here, and to have hidden from the law in the sooty cavity behind the fireplace of the Green Man Inn at Hatton. It's tempting to overemphasize Turpin's connection with Heathrow, when the unromantic truth is that there is little evidence to suggest he ever visited the place.

If caught, robbers were executed at Tyburn on the then edge of London, and sometimes the corpses were brought back to the Heath to be displayed as a deterrent to others. By the late eighteenth century the sight of these rotting remains began to offend an increasingly liberal upper class, and the practice was stopped.

With road improvements and an increase in traffic the highwayman's trade became increasingly risky, and the profession began to disappear. Away from the road, violence continued with prize fighting, and the Heath was a popular place for gentlemen to defend their honour in a duel. From time to time the army used this open space near London for big exercises and parades.

In 1784 the area played a key role in the history of map-making. Pioneer cartographer Major-General Roy measured a 5½-mile base line as part of a trigonometric survey. One end was near Heathrow, the other at Hampton. Roy marked the ends of his precisely measured line with wooden posts. The post near Heathrow was later replaced by a more durable marker – a cannon barrel set upright in the ground. In 1926, on the 200th birthday of this 'Father of the Ordnance Survey', a commemorative plaque was fixed above the cannon. Cannon and plaque were both removed for construction of the airport in 1944, but happily both have now been returned. They're close to their original site, in a corner a few feet north of the Northern Perimeter Road, to the east of the tunnel, next to the taxi feeder park.

As the airport today caters for the weary traveller, so the inns along the northern perimeter have been doing for two centuries. While to the south lies the road to the south-west, along here runs the A4 route to the west, the historic coach road to Bath. Through Colnbrook, Poyle and Longford there is a succession of coaching inns, many with large double doors big enough to allow horses to get to the stables at the rear, and even to admit coaches for safe keeping overnight. Here the travellers of the past, tired and hungry, would take refreshment and perhaps stay the night.

On the Bath Road, a hundred yards east of the tunnel, one of these inns still stands. Built in 1765, it has been called in turn 'The Three Pigeons', 'The Magpie and Pigeon', and now 'The Three Magpies'. It's still in business and you can get a cheap hot lunch here. None of the stables or associated buildings remain, and the old place is badly hemmed in by Heathrow police station. Before the airport was built, 'The Three Magpies' stood on a corner and marked the turning from relatively busy Bath Road to quiet Heathrow Road, which led to the village.

As in the rest of England, enclosure of wild land was gradually taking place over the centuries. Eventually Heathrow no longer stood on the edge of the heath, but was surrounded by orchards and fields of grain.

On 17 December 1903, in America, amongst the lonely sand dunes of Kill Devil Hill near Kitty Hawk on the coast of North Carolina, two sons of an Ohio bishop became the first men to achieve sustained and controlled flight. Orville Wright was carried 120 feet in a flight lasting twelve seconds. Later on that day his brother Wilbur also flew their fragile canvas aeroplane 'Flyer', and achieved 852 feet.

The Wright brothers were the first to fly because they had spent many hours practising gliding. When, as others had already done, they developed a fairly viable flying machine, they were alone in having the experience to fly theirs. The hard-working agricultural folk of Heathrow – if they knew of the Wright brothers – can scarcely have had a notion of how their village was to be affected.

The remains of the Celtic settlement with its defensive banks had by now become known as Shapsbury Hill, or occasionally Caesar's Camp, the latter name perpetuating a mistaken belief that the site was Roman and military. In 1906 the remains were almost levelled, and ploughed over. Even worse lay in store for this jewel in our archaeological heritage, as we shall see.

Meanwhile the plough and the hedgerow had taken their toll of most of the heath, to the extent that the only land left bearing the name Hounslow Heath consisted of a few acres south of the Roman road. Even this, though not actually cultivated, bore little resemblance to open heath. The army had long concentrated their parades and exercises here, and the military eventually monopolized it.

With the outbreak of the First World War in 1914, the army used Hounslow Heath as a training aerodrome for the Royal Flying Corps. For the first time the rustic population of Heathrow, two miles distant, regularly heard the sound of the new-fangled flying machines. It was eleven years since the Wright brothers had made man's first powered flight.

German airships became popularly feared. Bombing raids were thought to pose a major threat to Britain, and a crescent of defensive aerodromes was established around the southern edge of London. Hounslow Heath was at the western end of the crescent, and was made the headquarters of the group. At the airfields, fighter aircraft stood ready to scramble and intercept raiding Zeppelins, aiming to rupture their skins and so bring them down. At first the fighters used ordinary ammunition and even pointed instruments, both with little success, but when special combustible bullets were developed they were able to achieve devastating results.

Only just over a mile from Hounslow Heath, another airfield opened in 1917. Hanworth Aerodrome was used by the Whitehead factory in Feltham for testing and delivering their aircraft. When the War ended in 1918, Hanworth closed.

An anxious observer living in Heathrow at this time might have wondered if it was coincidence that two aerodromes had appeared within four miles of the village. Was it something to do with the ubiquitous flatness of the land? Its proximity to London? Were the two aerodromes going to be followed by any others?

The First World War brought into the wings one of the principal players of the Heathrow Story. Richard Fairey was born in 1887, the son of a once-rich timber merchant who died penniless. His Uncle Ben took it upon himself to look after the boy, although he didn't seem to have much affection for him. There is a story that one day Uncle Ben fell down a well. Young Richard is supposed to have declared 'Serves him right', not realizing that the unfortunate uncle was clinging to the bucket chain, still alive and still within earshot. Once hauled to the surface, Uncle Ben disinherited his nephew on the spot.

Richard got himself a miserable five-shillings-a-week office job with an arc lamp manufacturer in Holloway. He studied electrical engineering and chemistry at night school, and moved to Finchley Power Station as Assistant to the Manager. By now he had become interested in aviation and won prizes and gold medals from the Kite and Model Aeroplane Association. He sold the copyright for one of his models to Gamages department store, who paid him several hundred pounds. When John Dunne, the pioneer aeroplane builder, got in touch with Mr Fairey to complain that the Gamages model infringed one of his own copyrights, he was so impressed by the enthusiastic young man that he offered him a job. Fairey worked for John Dunne's company at Eastchurch on the Isle of Sheppey, where the aerodrome was shared with Short Brothers. In 1913 he joined Shorts as Chief Stress Man and progressed through Works Manager to Chief Engineer.

In 1915, at the age of twenty-eight, he started his own aeroplane company. The wartime government found him assembly space at Clayton Road in Hayes, three miles north of Heathrow. Here Fairey Aviation had to share space in the little factory of the Army Motor Lorries Company. The government supplied a workforce of Belgian refugees. In 1918 a new factory was built for Fairey at North Hyde Road in Hayes. We shall come back to the energetic Richard Fairey when he moves centre stage later in the story.

At the end of the war there were a lot of aeroplanes left with nothing much to do. People had become familiar with the idea of a flying machine and had developed sufficient confidence in their safety to want to try them out for themselves. Joy rides became a popular entertainment all over the country.

The aerodrome at Hounslow Heath was only a mile from the nearest Underground station at Hounslow West (or Hounslow Barracks as it was then). At weekends crowds of Londoners arrived on the tube and paid 1s 6d to visit the aerodrome, which was still guarded by the army. The local police even had to sort out traffic jams outside on the Roman road. The charge for a joy ride was £1 for fifteen minutes. One customer paid extra to have himself flown through Tower Bridge.

In July 1919 war restrictions were lifted to allow international civil flights, and just after 9 a.m. on 25 August genial Lieutenant Bill Lawford with his one passenger, an *Evening Standard* reporter, lifted off the grass runway at Hounslow, bound for Paris. Their wood and canvas First World War bomber, a DH4a, carried a cargo of newspapers, several brace of grouse, and a few jars of fresh Devonshire cream. This first British airline was called Aircraft Transport and Travel, and later in the same day the company chalked up a world first, when Major Cyril Patteson bumped across the same stretch of grass and heaved four passengers aloft in his DH16, also bound for Paris. This 2½-hour flight was the start of the world's first sustained daily international scheduled commercial air service. The passengers travelled in an enclosed cabin which was nevertheless draughty and bitterly cold, and the turbulent ride was far from stately.

The affairs of AT&T were themselves turbulent. Like other early airlines, they had trouble attracting enough passengers to stay in business. The journey to Paris relied heavily on good weather, so that the pilot could see the ground and navigate by referring to landmarks. Railway lines were particularly useful, and some Southern Railway stations even had their names painted in white paint on their roofs.

An aerodrome at Croydon, south of London, was, with other advantages, closer to continental destinations, and so a little cheaper for the struggling airlines to operate from. So at the end of March 1920 Hounslow Heath Customs Aerodrome closed, less than a year after it was declared open, and Croydon became the new London airport. Like Hounslow, the new site was right on a main road (the Brighton Road), and had been an anti-Zeppelin base. Peculiarly, it was at first bisected by a country lane which featured gates and a 'level crossing' for aeroplanes. By 1928 the lane was closed and the terminal moved to what was at the time a strikingly modern building on the east of the site, next to the Brighton Road. This elegant and exciting terminal, with its radio tower and its viewing platform on the roof, made a welcome change from the huts and makeshift buildings which had hitherto welcomed air travellers to the capital of the Empire. There was even a hotel built next to the terminal. This is how Britain's premier airport remained until the suspension of civil aviation in

1939 with the outbreak of the Second World War. Croydon never regained its position as the airport for London, as we shall see, but most of the airport buildings remain. The hangars and Imperial Airways workshops have become part of an industrial estate built on the apron. The Aerodrome Hotel is still in business. Most of the terminal building has been converted to offices, with the impressive entrance hall now serving as a warehouse. A fork lift truck beavers away where the privileged classes once proffered their air tickets.

The former airport buildings at Hounslow were burnt to the ground in 1929, and Hounslow Heath today is little more than a local recreation ground. Poignantly sited almost below the busy glide path into Heathrow's Runway 27 Left, this short-lived airport is today just somewhere to walk the dog. The only pointer to its former importance is a plaque mounted on a brick plinth opposite 'The Hussar' pub on the Roman road. This marks where the busy entrance used to be.

While Hounslow Heath went to seed and Croydon busied itself as the airport of London, life at Heathrow was carrying on much as in the preceding century. The houses had no electricity and most days were filled with hard work and little else. But in 1925 the twentieth century did come very near, with the opening of the Great West Road.

Britain's economy was growing almost as fast as car ownership, and the roads out of London had been exhibiting chronic congestion. The route to the west and south-west was a case in point – this was still basically the Roman road! Chiswick, Brentford and Hounslow, which had sprung up along this route, were by now so busy that the vitality of their high streets threatened to strangle the very thoroughfare which had given them life. It took too long to get into and out of London, and a bypass was embarked upon.

The Great West Road is today lined by houses throughout its length, and for a quarter of a century it has itself suffered the indignity of being bypassed, by the M4 motorway. But in its day it was the equivalent of our motorways. Wide and straight to an unprecedented degree, it was put through virgin countryside. The road symbolized all that was modern, and there was even excitement and glamour in the proud name Great West Road. The opening ceremony was performed by His Majesty King George V.

The road took traffic from Chiswick to a point on the Bath Road three miles from Heathrow, a point then outside the built-up area and associated traffic jams. The fruit and vegetables that were being grown in the area could now be speeded to Covent Garden market more efficiently.

A year later an extension was built for traffic to the south-west. The Great South West Road, now the start of the A30, rejoined the Roman road clear of the built-up area, at Bedfont, on its way passing within a mile of Heathrow. Both these great roads, and the rapid communications with Heathrow which they made possible, were to help shape the future.

Just off the Great West Road is the village of Heston, four miles closer to London than is Heathrow. The newly formed Airwork company of young Nigel Norman and Alan Muntz acquired 170 acres to the north-west of the village in September 1928, and work started on a super-modern aerodrome among the cabbage fields and fruit trees. Less than a year later, on 6 July 1929, Lord Thompson, the Air Minister, flew in to perform the opening ceremony.

A distinctive feature of Heston Aerodrome was that the tree-lined approach was exactly aligned with magnetic north, and the airport buildings at the top of the drive were planned rather in the shape of an arrow head. Seen from the air, drive and buildings together resembled an arrow pointing north. At the point of the arrow the Art Deco-inspired main airport building contained a restaurant, lounge, flight offices and the Heston Aero Club, the whole thing topped by the control tower. The two sides of the

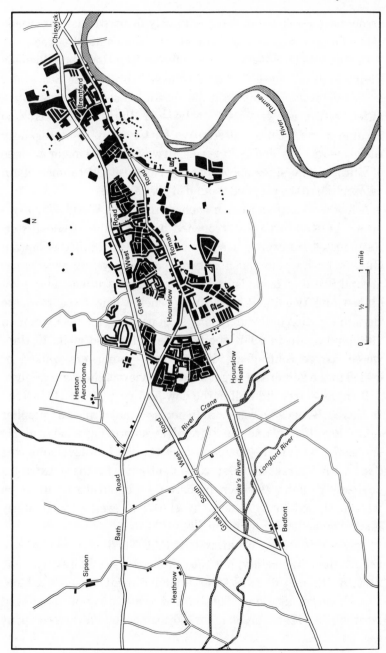

Heathrow and the roads into London, 1926

arrow head consisted of extraordinarily futuristic hangars made of reinforced concrete with spans of more than a hundred feet.

Heston was intended for private flying. The Household Brigade Flying club was based here, and the Airwork Flying School did brisk business. Eventually some scheduled services were introduced, to the Isle of Wight, Jersey and Blackpool. Heston also became a bad weather alternative for Croydon, so occasionally the place was invaded by Imperial Airways and the major airlines of Europe. The skies above nearby Heathrow were once again resounding to the prophetic sound of aero engines.

A few weeks after Heston opened, the First World War aerodrome at Hanworth was reopened by the Duke of Gloucester. Resurrected Hanworth was part of former Air Minister Captain Guest's masterplan for a network of twenty-two aerodromes around Britain. He envisaged each one having at least four aeroplanes and two instructors, in a scheme calculated to make Britain a nation of the air. Many local people remember when, in 1931 and again in 1932, the Graf Zeppelin paid visits to Hanworth. Large contingents of Heathrow youngsters walked or cycled to the aerodrome to get a close-up view of the giant airship.

Richard Fairey did well in the new factory in North Hyde Road in Hayes. By now he was established as a major aircraft supplier to the Royal Navy and the Fairey III was proving a particularly successful model. His company took the lead in developing the flap, with Fairey the first consistently to fit these extra-lift devices. The flap was important because it enabled aircraft which were designed to fly fast to fly slowly as well – particularly helpful when landing or taking off.

Fairey was testing his aircraft at RAF Northolt, three miles to the north of the factory, but the Air Force gave Fairey notice to quit by the end of 1929. This announcement came as a blow, though not a fatal one. The limited availability of hangars at Northolt had been a problem for some time, and Fairey's company was by now so busy that really it needed a test aerodrome of its own in any case. The RAF decision merely hastened the inevitable.

Brimming with boyish enthusiasm as ever, Dick Fairey set out to find another test site. He wanted somewhere with plenty of room for future expansion, a place where he could eventually move his assembly lines, so that assembly and testing would no longer be separated by a troublesome road journey. Ideally he wanted a site where one day he would be able to move the whole factory as well.

Four miles to the south of North Hyde Road, in the parish of Harmondsworth, the sleepy village of Heathrow seemed to have what he was after. The land here was flat, with good drainage and few buildings. Unlike Hayes, there was no railway within miles of Heathrow, and so no urban sprawl. Future expansion seemed to be no problem here. To top it all, the Great South West Road was only a mile away, offering excellent communications with London and the Fairey seaplane test site on the south coast.

In January 1929, Fairey purchased 150 acres at Heathrow from the vicar of Harmondsworth, and later in the year he snapped up neighbouring plots from others. No doubt some Heathrow residents were concerned about the environmental implications of Fairey's activities, but at least they could take comfort in the fact that his plans were for a test aerodrome, not an airport. Flights would rarely amount to more than a handful a week. The ceaseless and noisy comings and goings that Heston endured would not be experienced at Heathrow.

Fairey's aerodrome was known by several names. Sometimes it was 'Heathrow', sometimes 'Harmondsworth' and rather later 'The Great West Aerodrome'. Those who knew the place personally usually refer to it today as simply 'the Fairey aerodrome'.

In the north-east corner of his new airfield Fairey built a hangar which at the time was the largest of its type in the world.

The word FAIREY was painted in huge white capitals on the roof. In front of it was a concrete apron but, as with all aerodromes at this time, the airfield itself was indeed little more than a field. The grass surface was prepared by Hunters of Chester, using disc harrows and levellers, and it was kept in trim by a Pennsylvania tractor pulling seven 16-inch mowers in such a way that the mowers overlapped to produce a perfectly clean swathe. *Flight* magazine described the surface at this 'remarkable aerodrome' as being 'like a billiard table', and went on to describe an experiment in which a car crossed the field 'at 58 m.p.h. without experiencing the slightest bump'. Some classic aircraft were destined to be developed here, including the Gordon and the Seal, the Fox bomber and the Firefly single seater. There was the highly versatile Swordfish, and the precocious Hendon monoplane night bomber. The celebrated Fairey long-range monoplane – with its seemingly endless wingspan – was tested here before going on to win for Britain the world distance record.

Aircraft were brought from North Hyde Road by lorry. Aeroplanes were still relatively small and light, often consisting of little more than wood, canvas and wire. Usually they were towed backwards on their own wheels, but sometimes the whole thing was lifted on to the back of a flat lorry. The fixing of the wings to the fuselage took place at the aerodrome. Typically there would be about six aircraft at Heathrow, and about thirty employees.

Flying at the Great West Aerodrome consisted mainly of delivery and test flights. The deliveries were one-way journeys from Faireys to their customers. Test flights were more frequent and consisted of two types. Firstly, all aircraft leaving the production line were flown extensively to make thoroughly sure that they worked properly. Secondly, and more excitingly, there were development flights when experimental models would be put through their paces for the first time. Test pilot observations from such flights would suggest modifications, then the aircraft would be flown again, suggesting another round of modifications, and so on, until eventually the basic design would be honed to the optimum.

Most of the design was done at Hayes, but the modifications that could be made quickly between flights were designed at the aerodrome. There was a two-storey white-painted office building on either side of the hangar door, and on the top floor of one of these was a little drawing office where these local modifications were detailed. In 1935 a 21-year-old Cambridge graduate cycled down the country lanes from Hayes, past the blossoming orchards of Heathrow, and arrived to start work at this office for the first time. Young Peter Masefield stayed with Fairey for two years, before going on to become a leading figure in British aviation. He was destined to return to Heathrow as the man in charge, thirty years later.

In 1935 Mr Fairey staged a garden party at his aerodrome for the Royal Aeronautical Society, of which he was a former President. 1,500 members and guests turned up on the idyllic hot summer's day, to watch aircraft overhead, to examine them on the ground, to wander amongst the trade stands in the hangar, and of course to take tea.

Edward, Prince of Wales, was a keen flyer. In his Fairey III F he often used Smith's Lawn, which was handy for Fort Belvedere, his modest house in Windsor Great Park. If Smith's Lawn was waterlogged after a lot of rain, he landed at Northolt. If that too was bogged, which it often was, he sometimes resorted to the privately owned Great West Aerodrome. It was six months after Edward became King in January 1936 that the King's Flight was formed to provide the Royal Family with air transport. 'Mouse' Fielden, the King's favourite pilot, was named Captain of the King's Flight and promoted to Wing Commander. In the summer the King and Mrs Wallis Simpson went on holiday aboard a yacht on the Mediterranean. The King shocked onlookers by appearing

in shorts and even without a shirt. All the time the love of the
King and Head of the Church of England for the divorced com-
moner Mrs Simpson presented him with an agonizing dilemma: if
he married he would have to relinquish the throne. When the
highly publicized holiday could be prolonged no more, the
troubled King returned to the United Kingdom by aeroplane and
landed at Heathrow. He was expected at Hendon Aerodrome to
the north of London, but to avoid ceremony the King slipped into
the sleepy Great West Aerodrome. With Mouse Fielden at the
controls, he landed unobserved at 6.30 p.m. and was whisked
away by car, out of the aerodrome gates, down Cain's Lane, along
the Great South West Road and on past Staines to Fort Belvedere.
After less than an hour there he was driven to London to face his
mother over dinner at Buckingham Palace. We can only guess
what the old lady had to say about her easy-going son's semi-nude
appearances with Mrs Simpson, which had been front paged by
the world's press. Three months later Edward VIII abdicated to
marry the woman he loved.

The 1935 Royal Aeronautical Society garden party had been
such a success that the event was repeated in 1936. It then
became a highly enjoyable annual fixture, although the English
weather tried hard to prevent this. In 1937 drizzle and low cloud
made it almost impossible to see the aeroplanes. The 1939 gathering was lashed by torrential rain although it had been mislead-
ingly sunny until half an hour before the show, so that everyone
was fooled into coming in thin summer clothes.

The event always remained an exclusive one. A suggestion of a
public enclosure on the far side of the field was never taken up,
and the prestigious 5/- tickets were only ever available through
members. The RAeS felt there were already ample flying events
which catered for the general public, and that their successful
garden parties were best left alone. The reception line which
greeted arrivals preserved the garden party mood, although

upwards of 4,000 guests might file past. The star of the flying displays was Chris Staniland, Fairey's top test pilot. During the show there was a loudspeaker commentary by the aviation correspondent of the *Evening Standard*, but at tea time this gave way to an orchestra which played Gilbert and Sullivan and the fashionable tunes of Cole Porter. The 'nuts and bolts' stands in the hangar advertised everything from propellers and wheels to engines and fire-fighting devices. The aircraft lined up for inspection on the grass were largely latest models, everything from the modest airliners of those days to glamorous fighters, with a few nostalgic oddities for good measure. For the ladies the garden parties were primarily a social function, the Ascot of aviation, attended by all the aeronautical world and its wife.

As the sodden assembly of 1939 peered out from the shelter of the crowded marquees, they were witnessing the gathering storm clouds of war. Hitler's invasion of Poland was only weeks away, and the industry had been gripped by a dreadful urgency. A formation of twelve of the new monoplane Spitfire fighters droned by overhead, just below the black cloud. Amongst the sea of upturned faces was that of the Air Minister himself, Sir Kingsley Wood, his serious countenance adding to the foreboding at what was to be the last garden party at the Great West Aerodrome. With him was the Under Secretary of State for Air, First World War fighter ace Harold Balfour. Like his boss, Balfour was preoccupied with boosting air power to counter the mighty Luftwaffe but, as we shall see, he also had an eye for the civil aviation potential of Heathrow.

Away from the aerodrome, events in the village were more down to earth. In 1935 a sewage farm occupying several acres was built at Perry Oaks, on the western edge of the community. The main product of the works – dried sludge – became popular as a cheap and potent fertilizer, and farmers fetched it by the cartload.

Heathrow was blessed with some of the finest soil in England.

Easy to dig brick earth, it had been classified Grade One by the Ministry of Agriculture, putting Heathrow in the top 5 per cent of the nation's land. Besides bountiful orchard and cereal crops, the area specialized in market gardening, supplying London with prodigious amounts of fruit and vegetables. Steam traction engines, horses and carts and petrol lorries nightly took the Great West Road to deliver this produce to Covent Garden market.

The village was one of the most rural spots within an easy drive of London. The quiet turning off the Bath Road at 'The Three Magpies' was called Heathrow Road, and it led into a different world of peace and tranquillity. Here on the approach to Heathrow local children could set up stumps in the middle of the road and rarely have their cricket disturbed by more than a passing bicycle.

The lovely cornfields, apple orchards and strips of brassicas were punctuated by an occasional flooded gravel pit, most of them about a hundred feet across. These old workings had matured into delightful reed-fringed ponds which were havens for a rich variety of wildlife. Many were full of trout, and attracted kingfishers. The one behind 'The Three Magpies' had an island in it. All were popular for swimming in summer, skating in winter.

By the 1930s a copse had grown up around Roy's Cannon. The famous marker was surrounded by respectful railings but it still became overgrown occasionally, despite being the responsibility of the Ministry of Works.

The biggest farm in Heathrow was that of the Philps family, a name familiar in the district for generations. They ran their substantial tracts from Heathrow Hall, an elegant country home set in mature trees. Like most of the buildings on Heathrow Road, it was on the right or west side, looking across the road to fields which had once been the edge of Hounslow Heath. It is tempting to suppose that it was this arrangement of a row of houses by the heath which gave the place its name.

Next along the lane from Heathrow Hall was Palmer's Farm, parts of it dating from the seventeenth century. In the last years of the village a brickyard sprang up opposite this farm. The brick earth of the district was indeed excellent for making bricks.

Another hundred yards or so further along was a signpost on a triangle of grass in the middle of the road. Here at Wheatcut Corner the lane forked. Bearing slightly to the left was Cain's Lane, while more sharply to the right Heathrow Road continued.

Cain's Lane first. It was a mile long, and straight as an arrow. On the left, Wild's Farm was a nursery specializing in tulips, carnations and other flowers, many of them reared under glass. A couple of water towers were a landmark. Two generations of the Wild family lived side by side here, with the newer house a 1927 mock-Tudor building. A few yards down the lane was a primitive Methodist chapel. This corrugated iron mission hall was the nearest thing to a church that Heathrow had. A Sunday school was held here, as well as services on Sunday mornings and evenings, at which the congregation of ten or twenty was accompanied by a harmonium. Opposite, an orchard bordered the Great West Aerodrome, which had two separate gateways on to the lane. Beyond the aerodrome was Cain's Farm, and then the Great South West Road cut across before the lane finally ended at Hatton Road. This last section of Cain's Lane still exists today, with its original name. It's now a suburban residential road. North of the A30 only a few yards of Cain's Lane has been retained, as an emergency access to the airport. It leads from a check-point at the perimeter to a taxiway near the Pan Am maintenance base. Beyond that taxiway Cain's Lane has been obliterated.

Back at Wheatcut Corner, the right fork formed the continuation of Heathrow Road, past Perrott's Farm and the village's only pub, 'The Plough and Harrow'. The beer and cider on offer here rarely attracted more than a handful of customers. Some of the twenty or so workers at the brickworks used the Plough at lunchtime, but there was little passing trade. The landlord was an ex-policeman named Mr Basham.

After seventeenth-century Heathrow Farm on the right, and a pond particularly rich in trout on the left, Heathrow Road passed the poorest homes in the community. Wretched little huts of weatherboard and thatch, they dotted the north side of the road as far as Perry Oaks. This stretch bore an unlikely resemblance to the backwoods of the USA. The occupants of these wooden houses often had no teeth. Those that did have them often used them for chewing tobacco. Miss Harbour, who played the mission hall harmonium, also snorted snuff. The people living at the The Magpies or Harmondsworth considered themselves posh by comparison.

At the west end of Heathrow was Perry Oaks. Here was the junction with Tithe Barn Lane, and yet another picturesque pond. The Perry Oaks house itself was partly Elizabethan, making it the oldest house in Heathrow. Occasionally its residents must have suffered when the prevailing wind evoked the expanding sewage farm with its growing number of murky lagoons a few hundred yards further west.

Running south from the centre of the village, High Tree Lane passed the Sherwood poultry farm and went on to cross Duke's River by a ford. This Goathouse Tree Ford, as it was referred to on maps, was usually about eighteen inches deep. It was the centre of something of a local resort, because a popular path ran off along the south bank of the river from here. As well as Heathrow people, families used to walk here from as far as Sipson to bathe and picnic.

One of the big events of the Heathrow calendar was the annual ploughing match. The local school on Bath Road had a half day and the villagers organized side shows and a vegetable competition. The match itself had classes for both tractors and teams of horses, but over the years the tractors inevitably began to pre-dominate. By the time of the last event, on the eve of war in 1939, there were very few hoofed competitors left.

A mile east of Heathrow, also down a narrow turning off the Bath Road, lay the village of Hatton. By far the biggest and most impressive house here was The Gore. It was flanked by a row of more modest residences with names like The Lilacs and The Cedars. Hatton residents tended to be more sophisticated than folk at Heathrow. Some were lucky enough to have a job at 'The Gram' – the HMV record factory in Hayes. As well as a pub called 'The Dog and Partridge' there was a small shop. This amenity was highly valued in a community where buses were unknown and a bicycle was a luxury.

Heathrow lay within the parish of Harmondsworth, a bigger village two miles to the north west. It's a tribute to the planners that Harmondsworth remains remarkably well preserved today. Part of Greater London, almost surrounded by motorways, increasingly threatened by airport buildings, hotels and peripheral industries, it nevertheless retains its village green, its church and its two quiet pubs. Everybody knows everybody else there. The village is still surrounded by open fields intensively cultivated for market produce. At Harmondsworth today we can get some idea of what Heathrow was like before they built the airport.

# 2
# War

The crowd at Heston Aerodrome had been gathering for most of the afternoon, blocking the narrow country lanes that led to the airfield. Many people had got soaking wet in the heavy rain which had just stopped. Diplomats from France, Germany and Italy, British cabinet ministers, the world's press, newsreel film crews, the Lord Mayor of London – all were present. At 5.38 p.m. there were excited shouts as a distant aircraft was sighted. At first it was just a tiny speck moving against the grey sky, but within a couple of minutes the small Lockheed 14 airliner had touched down on the grass field and taxied to a halt.

The Prime Minister, Neville Chamberlain, appeared in the cabin door, smiling and waving his hat. The crowd rushed forward to greet and congratulate him. He stepped down to a waiting cluster of microphones.

'This morning I had another talk with the German Chancellor, Herr Hitler, and here is a paper which bears his name upon it, as well as mine.'

He held the paper aloft before reading from it the joint declaration. This brought further enthusiastic cheering, which continued as the police cleared a way for the Prime Minister to reach his car. He was driven slowly towards the exit amidst a rousing rendition of 'For He's A Jolly Good Fellow'. The long driveway down to the main gate was lined by 120 cheering Eton schoolboys, who had of their own initiative asked for permission to welcome their victorious Prime Minister. Outside the gates further crowds of grateful citizens cheered Chamberlain on his way to Downing Street.

The events of that wet afternoon of 30 September 1938, playing themselves out only three miles from sleepy Heathrow, were of enormous importance to Britain, indeed the world. Chamberlain had flown to meet Hitler three times in September in an attempt to avert war. The Nazi dictator had demanded that neighbouring Czechoslovakia cede the Sudetenland to Germany, and by their appeasement Chamberlain and France's Daladier had left the Czechs defenceless against the advancing German war machine. History judges Chamberlain an ostrich with his head in the sand, but some people credit him with at least gaining time for Britain to rearm. The question remains whether Hitler would have curtailed his expansion if Chamberlain had stood up to him at those September meetings.

While Britain made hurried preparations for the possibility of war, civilian business carried on and the Air Ministry concerned itself not only with the RAF, but with making plans for civil aviation as well. There was a growing realization that Croydon was getting too small for the larger airliners that were now flying. Since there was little room to expand the aerodrome, which was in any case poorly sited on the side of a hill, Sir Archibald Sinclair and his department looked for somewhere bigger. Sir Archibald freely admitted that he didn't know one end of a plane from the other, and it was his Under-Secretary of State, Harold Balfour, who put most of the energy into solving the problem. Since his adventures as a fighter pilot in the First World War, Balfour had combined politics with running various airlines, and he was a passionate champion of civil aviation. He urged that Heston should be developed as the new London Airport.

Balfour likes to recount his uncanny introduction to Heston. In the mid-1920s he had been flying solo in his Cirrus II Moth when he had got lost. To find out where he was he touched down in a field near the junction of the Great West Road and the Bath Road. An AA scout saw him land and came over for a chat, telling him he was near a place called Heston and that here would surely be a flying field in the future. Balfour thought little more of this conversation until he had cause to remember the AA man when Norman and Muntz opened Heston Aerodrome three or four years later.

The Cabinet agreed that Heston should be expanded, and that it should handle all the bigger aircraft. It would be complemented by a ring of lesser airports around London, all controlled by a London Airports Authority rather on the lines of the Port of London Authority. The first step in realizing this plan was the Air Ministry (Heston and Kenley Aerodromes Extension) Act, more conveniently referred to as the Heston Extension Act. It gave the Government powers to acquire certain lands and stop up local roads, including Southall Lane and part of Cranford Lane and High Street. The aerodrome was to be extended to the west and south-west, and the local vicarage was one of the buildings which stood in its way. The act promised at great length that the vicar would be provided with an equivalent house, and three acres of land, within the parish. The part of the act dealing with Kenley gave powers to expand that aerodrome to become one in the ring around London. Kenley is south of London, a few miles further out than Croydon.

The Heston Extension Act received the Royal Assent on 4 August 1939, one of the last bills to pass into law before the outbreak of the Second World War. It probably caused concern to the few residents of Heathrow with enough leisure time to worry about noise levels, because it now looked as if the main airport of London would soon be operating three miles from their homes. In the event Adolph Hitler intervened on 1 September, with his attack on Poland. Two days later Britain declared war, and the Air Ministry's plans for Heston were put to one side.

At first the Second World War was barely distinguishable from peacetime, but the months of the 'phoney war' soon passed. Most of Europe fell to Hitler, and U-boats began to sink Allied merchant ships in an attempt, amongst other things, to starve Britain. Agriculture became part of the battle to survive, and Heathrow, with its precious fertility, was in the front line.

Over at Hatton the war years were enlivened by a detachment of Guards, who took over The Gore. They brought electricity to Hatton for the first time.

On the Bath Road between Heathrow and Harmondsworth, Professor Barnes Wallis worked in secret on his 'bouncing bombs' project. The professor spent months here at the Road Research Laboratory, experimenting with scale models of the Möhne Dam. The final tests were carried out at a disused Welsh dam before the actual raid by the RAF Dambusters successfully bounced Wallis' spinning spherical bombs across the water to their target, with results which would have impressed Noah.

The war introduced widespread hard runways. Until now aerodromes had often had concrete aprons, but the runways had almost without exception remained grass. Concrete runways had been thought too expensive, and some experts even pronounced them 'too hard'. Heavier aircraft had tended to be flying boats because heavy land planes sank into the mud when using a grass runway after rain. This could cause the undercarriage to collapse, and it invariably left deep ruts which, hardened by the sun, constituted a hazard to other aircraft taking off and landing. Opinion now started to drift away from flying boats, but still the majority view remained in their favour. After all, long-distance routes throughout the world were geared to flying boats. From Southampton to Sydney, areas of water were kept unobstructed for them to land. At many places there were no facilities for land planes. With the flying boat, aviation could expand into any primitive and hostile corner of the world, simply by finding a calm stretch of water.

Even in the midst of war, civil schemes were being hatched. The Port of London Authority wanted a piece of the aviation action, and they campaigned for Government backing for a combined sea and air port on the Cliffe Marshes, on the south side of the Thames estuary, about thirty miles from the centre of London. The PLA idea was to bring together at Cliffe a port for ships, hard runways for land planes, and a circular non-tidal salt water lagoon, of some seven square miles, for flying boats.

Harold Balfour also found time to look ahead to the civil aviation needs of peacetime. As Secretary of State for Air with special responsibility for civil aviation, he and a depleted civil aviation staff at the Ministry spent odd moments looking at the possibilities. Transport aircraft were getting a lot bigger and more numerous in the forcing house of war, and they were demanding longer and longer runways. Even an expanded Heston now looked as if it would be too small. The main war-time airports that could handle these large aircraft were away from London, at Whitchurch near Bristol and Prestwick in Scotland. Balfour realized that London was going to need a new super-airport, and he gradually concluded that Heathrow was the only place for it.

He spent many hours with a large-scale map of London and the surrounding countryside. He had a celluloid grid cut out to represent the area required, and he slid this grid around the map. He found only one undeveloped site both close to the centre of London and able to accommodate the necessary 4,500 acres, or seven square miles. Heathrow.

In February 1943 Balfour set down his thoughts about airports in a minute to his Permanent Under-Secretary, Sir Arthur Street. There were four main points:

1 Heston is now obsolete as a site for our biggest aircraft.

2 We should explore the possibilities of Heathrow and anywhere else with room for the aerodrome of the dimensions we now require, plus a margin for the future.

3 Britain will require three airports for transoceanic aircraft and I suggest Prestwick, Liverpool and London. It's unlikely all three will be fogged-in at the same time.

4 We cannot build now because of war-time shortages of men and materials. Further, if we do build now, and the war continues, there will be further rapid advances in aviation, and our work will quickly become as out of date as our Heston scheme appears to us now.

During 1943 the war swung the way of the Allies and it began to look as if the defeat of Germany was only a matter of time. The senior staffs turned their attention to the needs of what they termed Stage Two of the war – the defeat of Japan. Balfour now saw his chance and took it. He and Sir Arthur Street prepared a paper which the Air Minister then took to Cabinet. The paper argued that a big new RAF base was needed at Heathrow for Transport Command to reach the Far East with men and supplies. The Cabinet appointed a committee to look at this question, and Balfour represented the Air Ministry on it.

The Under-Secretary of State deliberately set out to deceive this committee. Balfour knew perfectly well that there were a number of existing airfields in the Home Counties that could supply the Far East, yet he told them a new airfield at Heathrow was essential. His real purpose was to get the super-airport that he knew London would need after the war. He felt the economic case for having such an airport to be so overwhelming that it justified his dishonest means of getting it.

This extraordinary confidence in his own judgement verged on ruthlessness. As a fighter pilot in the first war, Balfour exhibited this same quality when he attacked a German observer held aloft by a balloon. When the observer used his parachute, Balfour fired off the best part of a hundred rounds at his helpless dangling victim, killing him. This outraged his comrades, who condemned it as unsporting, but Balfour rationally pointed out that observers directed shells on to our trenches. They were skilled men who should not be allowed to float to earth and return to their deadly work. Similarly in the case of Heathrow, Balfour coolly justifies his actions and admits to no sense of guilt. He was the Minister in charge of civil aviation, therefore he was all for anything that would help civil aviation.

Also on the committee was Lord Beaverbrook, whom Balfour took into his confidence. The Beaver agreed to play along and support Balfour's assertion that the war effort simply could not do without an airfield at Heathrow. There were objections, particularly from Rob Hudson, representing the Ministry of Agriculture, and Ernie Brown, Health, but these men were not in a position to argue with Balfour's and Beaverbrook's expertise on the need for the new airfield. Neither could they offer any alternative site, so the committee concluded in favour of the scheme, and that recommendation was endorsed by the Cabinet.

The Cabinet were swayed by an appreciation of the peace-time value to the nation of a big airport close to London, and they were also aware of the project's personal benefit to themselves. The Government had repeatedly asked the Air Staff for a new London terminus for VIPs travelling from the centre of Government to Burma, the Far East and America. At that time long road and rail journeys preceded flights to these places. How tempting, then, to sanction a scheme which would introduce transoceanic flights from a place only a thirty-minute drive from Westminster.

Using emergency war-time powers, the Air Ministry were able to requisition the land they wanted, and work on the new airfield started in early 1944. Harold Balfour's tactics had succeeded in bypassing normal civilian procedures. In peace time, planning enquiries for a project of this size might have dragged on for years, with the result unpredictable at the end of it all.

Most of the village and the surrounding fields were compulsorily purchased, including the Fairey airfield. Richard Fairey himself was conveniently out of the way, serving as Secretary of the British Supply Council in Washington. He was outraged that his company, busy supplying the Fleet Air Arm, should be kicked out for what he probably saw was a trumped-up reason. He reluctantly agreed to share Heston with the RAF, a far cry from having his own test facility. The disruption caused to Fairey Aviation was severe, and it probably contributed to the subsequent decline of the company. Arguments between Fairey and the Government about compensation were not finally settled for twenty years, by which time Fairey had been taken over by Westland Helicopters.

The compulsory purchases dealt a blow that was shattering to most residents. Heathrow was all that they knew. Many families had lived there for generations, seldom travelling far from the village. Some residents came to look upon events as a sign from God that they should move; others were bitter.

While Balfour was passing off the new airport as a military scheme, the potential of Heathrow was spotted, apparently quite independently, by Brigadier-General A.C. Critchley, the new Director-General of the British Overseas Airways Corporation. BOAC had been established by the Government in 1939, to take over Imperial Airways and the old British Airways. General Critchley was not happy running the national airline as long as it was banished to the aerodrome at Whitchurch, 120 miles from the capital. An outstanding amateur golfer, the General commuted daily from his home near Sunningdale golf club to the BOAC head office in Victoria. The journey took him along the Great South West Road, past Heathrow. With BOAC's lack of a base near London weighing constantly on his mind, it was not long before he noticed the flat countryside he was passing, and put the two things together. This could be the new home for BOAC!

He stopped the car and explored on foot. Every morning for a week the General walked all around Heathrow, measuring distances and studying the terrain. As he describes in his 1961 autobiography, Critchley told the Air Ministry about his idea, and got Sir Archibald Sinclair's Permanent Secretary to join him on one of his perambulations. It is not clear whether the Permanent Secretary let Critchley know that Harold Balfour already had this very matter well in hand. Certainly in his book the General gives no hint of being aware of Balfour's Cabinet intrigues.

In March General Critchley called a press conference and told reporters:

'The first thing I did when I came into this Corporation and realized that it was homeless, was to look for one. I have found it. Only twelve and a half miles from Hyde Park Corner there is an ideal site for an airport for London covering 2,800 acres. It is 300 acres larger than Idlewild, the world's largest airport now being constructed sixteen miles from New York. An airport on these lines would be the finest advertisement this country could have. I can tell you about it: but I cannot tell you where it is – yet.'

Critchley also told pressmen that the principal runway would be 5,000 yards long, and that there would be a water runway for flying boats 4,000 yards long and 200 yards wide.

His motive for giving this slightly misleading account of things is not clear. Partly, perhaps, he wished to increase his own stature by showing himself to be the father of Heathrow Airport, a title which properly belongs to Balfour. Perhaps he wanted to hurry things along at Heathrow by raising public expectations, bringing pressure on the Government to transfer Heathrow for use as a great civil airport. This, after all, would allow his airline to get the London base it desperately lacked.

Some account of the press conference was carried by most dailies on 14 March 1944. Three months later, on 12 June, the *Daily Telegraph* suddenly presented a remarkable, unofficial and in places wildly exaggerated account of developments on the ground:

LONDON AIRPORT IS BEING BUILT NEAR STAINES

HUNDREDS OF ACRES TAKEN OVER: FIVE-MILE RUNWAY

Today I watched London's new post-war airport, which is to be the biggest in the world, taking shape.

Scores of lorries swept down a road closed to traffic. Bulldozers, special plough and levelling rakes were preparing a runway which, some people estimate, will be as long as five miles . . .

Hounslow West Underground Station, the nearest rail centre, is likely to be extended to the airfield, thus providing easy access to and from London.

Brigadier-General A. C. Critchley, Director-General of BOAC, gave a hint of the location of the new airport a short time ago when he spoke of a place 'within twelve and a half miles of Hyde Park'.

All very surprising for what was supposed to be another RAF station. It must have made interesting reading for the members of the Cabinet committee who had heard Balfour testify about the airfield's important military purpose.

Although none of the planned runways measured up to even half of the rather preposterous five miles quoted in the *Telegraph*, the work undertaken at Heathrow was nevertheless on a Herculean scale. Three runways were embarked upon, each one a staggering three hundred feet wide, and made out of 12-inch thick concrete cast *in situ* on a 24-inch base of gravel. They were built to handle any plane in existence, and in fact they could handle any plane built since. They are so wide that it would take a running athlete a quarter of a minute to cross one, or, put another way, fifteen days for an energetic snail.

The numerous flooded gravel pits had to be pumped dry and filled in. Some of them were still being filled in after runway construction had started. Any suitable material that came to hand was used for the job. Each pit was filled with nine inches of material, then compacted, then another nine inches, and so on.

A total of about 2,000,000 square yards of concrete were to be laid for runways and taxiways. In the event of heavy rain, vast quantities of water which, before construction, would have been absorbed by the ground, would now be collected by the hard surface, and it all had to be disposed of somehow. Calculations showed that if it was dumped into the Longford and Duke's Rivers it would cause a flood. Even the larger River Crane, a mile to the east of the site, could not take all the water in one go. So it was decided to arrange things so that rain water could be released gradually into the Crane. Large ponds or 'balancing reservoirs' were readied close to the river, and these tanks are still used today to hold the water until the level of the Crane is low enough to take it. Then it is gradually released into the stream. The two reservoirs – behind high wire fencing on either side of the A312 – are protected from stagnation by big thrashers which churn up the surface and allow oxygen into the water, preventing discoloration and smell.

The runway in the north of the airfield was built right across the remains of the Celtic settlement known as Caesar's Camp. These ruins had by now been largely obliterated, but nevertheless they constituted one of the most important ancient sites in Britain. Their destruction was a tragedy. Although the country was at war, a hasty archaeological dig was arranged before the Celtic settlement was excavated for foundations and covered with concrete. This same runway also went over King's Arbour and the end of Roy's base line, so the famous commemorative cannon was removed.

In October, Prime Minister Winston Churchill took the civil aviation department of the Air Ministry and made it into a

Ministry in its own right. Now, confusingly, there was both a Ministry of Civil Aviation and an Air Ministry. The man Churchill picked to run Civil Aviation was not Harold Balfour, who for six years had handled civil matters as Under-Secretary of State at the Air Ministry. Instead Churchill chose another Conservative, Lord Swinton, and Balfour packed his bags to become Resident Minister in West Africa. As far as important civil aviation decisions were concerned it was all over for the man who had paved the way for Heathrow Airport.

Would Lord Swinton's appointment affect plans for Heathrow? Would the new Minister decide that an intercontinental land plane base close to London was undesirable or unnecessary? Would he instead support a marine flying boat base? The BOAC fleet still consisted of a large number of flying boats, and it was widely felt that flying boats might yet dominate long-haul routes, particularly transatlantic. The two great airports of New York – La Guardia and Idlewild – were both being provided with facilities for flying boats.

In December the Conservative MP for Maidstone rose in the House of Commons and asked whether the Air Minister would indicate that there was not going to be a new civilian airport at Staines. Sir Archibald Sinclair replied that the airfield was being constructed for military purposes. The Member for Maidstone was not discouraged, and asked if a fast rail connection was possible.

'I am only concerned with the military aspect', insisted Sir Archibald, conceding only that rail would be a consideration when judging suitability for civilian use.

In January 1945 it was the turn of the Civil Aviation Minister to make an airports policy announcement. He ᴠ ld Scottish MPs that the RAF transatlantic base at Prestwick in Scotland would not be developed into Britain's principal airport. Heathrow was looking more and more likely to play this role. There was no sign of anything being done about either the PLA plan for Cliffe Marshes, or any other scheme.

Two days after Germany surrendered on 8 May 1945, Lord Swinton chaired a meeting of Ministry officials and airline chiefs at Ariel House, home of the Ministry of Civil Aviation. The subject of the meeting: short-term policy for London airports. Lord Swinton began by outlining the current situation. The Government had now decided that Heathrow should become the principal London airport as quickly as possible. To cope with the expected volume of traffic, it would have to be equipped with sets of parallel runways. Because of the construction work, Heathrow would not be available for civil use for some time. Therefore other London airport facilities would be needed for two or three years. The Prime Minister had ruled that civil and military aircraft must share facilities wherever necessary. The airline representatives then gave their views about the choice of a stop-gap until Heathrow was ready. They unanimously rejected Croydon, condemning its lack of hard runways, its small size and its dangerous topography. The meeting concluded that the only short-term alternative to Heathrow was Northolt. This was the RAF station used by Fairey Aviation before the building of the Great West Aerodrome. During the war Northolt had been equipped with hard runways which, though adequate for most types, were too short for transoceanic aircraft.

A Labour government replaced the 1945 caretaker government of Churchill on 23 May. Lord Winster replaced Lord Swinton as Minister of Civil Aviation.

On 13 August the new Labour Minister of Civil Aviation called another meeting to discuss the London airports. Lord Winster told the assembled airline bosses that the RAF had declined to provide them with facilities at Northolt. As a result the Minister had decided to rush Heathrow into use as soon as possible. Flying and building at Heathrow would therefore be concurrent. Not one of the three runways then planned for Heathrow was yet complete. The meeting considered the short-term options once again, this time at great length. One by one the options were found lacking:

Croydon. No hard runways. Small. Unsafe at night. Hangars too small.

Fairlop. Poor access from London. Fog.

Matching. 34 miles from London. Lack of housing for staff.

Bovingdon. 1½ hours from London. Low cloud.

Hatfield. Used by de Havilland for testing.

Gatwick. Bad drainage. Too close to the railway and road.

Gravesend. 25 miles. Airfield falls away towards river and west.

Redhill. Surrounding hills.

Radlett. One short runway. Bad approach.

Hornchurch. Bad weather.

Biggin Hill. Too small.

White Waltham, Bad access.

Black Bushe. On common land, therefore tenure limited.

The airlines urged strong representations at the highest level for the civil use of Northolt. For the minority of flights that could not be fitted into Northolt they suggested Hurn, near Bournemouth.

When the surrender of Japan finally ended the war , RAF Heathrow was left without a credible military role. Still the construction work went on.

# 3
# Concrete, Mud and Tents

Within weeks of the Japanese surrender, the Ministry of Civil Aviation appointed a panel of experts to probe the possibilities at RAF Heathrow, and to report how the concrete which had already set could best be adapted for civil purposes. The title of this London Airport Advisory Layout Panel was the first instance of the Ministry referring to Heathrow as 'London Airport'.

Although Heathrow was increasingly recognized as a civilian project, officially it remained military for the time being. In October the RAF sent an advance party of five officers and a hundred men to be based at the new airfield.

Flying boats had regularly crossed the Atlantic before the war, but the first commercial scheduled crossing by a land plane occurred when American Overseas Airways introduced a DC-4 service from New York to Hurn, via Gander and Shannon. The inaugural flight left New York on 23 October, and arrived 23 hours and 43 minutes later. The same journey by sea took five days. The AOA flight served to illustrate the arrival of a new generation of transoceanic land planes. Getting a London airport capable of handling them suddenly seemed all the more important.

One of the giant figures in the history of Heathrow was the Australian, Air Vice-Marshal Donald Clifford Tyndall Bennett, DSO, CBE, CB. Brought up on a remote farm on the edge of the outback, Don Bennett was undistinguished academically until he was smitten by an enthusiasm for aeroplanes. He talked his way into the RAAF and transferred to the RAF, working long hours to continue to upgrade his qualifications, particularly in navigation. Still in his twenties, he joined Imperial Airways, the forerunner of BOAC , and captained a flying boat. In a special two-seater with fuel tanks in the floats, he broke the world seaplane distance record with a flight from Scotland to South Africa. In the Second World War his brilliant career continued when he formed the Atlantic Ferry Organization. Ignoring the advice of countless experts, he personally demonstrated that it was possible to fly the North Atlantic in winter, and to bring to Britain desperately needed American aircraft. Going once again against the advice of other experts, he saw the need for a specialist group to mark targets in Germany for British bombers, and formed the famous Pathfinder Force. Operating Lancasters and wooden Mosquitoes, Pathfinder Force was an immediate success. Its superior pilots and navigators dropped coloured incendiaries and flares with great accuracy, picking out targets for the main bomber force which followed behind.

With peace in sight, the Air Vice-Marshal resigned from the RAF to head a new airline started by a consortium of shipping companies. He was just thirty-five years old. The company started as British Latin American Airways but Bennett quickly changed its name to British South American Airways when he found out that the former initials spelt a rude word in Spanish. BSAA was the first British airline to serve South America.

As its managing director, Bennett attended the meetings in Whitehall to discuss the future of London's airports. While BOAC and the American airlines claimed Hurn, there seemed to be nowhere for BSAA to go while Heathrow was being readied. Resourceful as ever, Bennett persuaded the building contractor at Heathrow, Wimpey, to allow BSAA to use the future London airport ahead of the competition, although still only one of the three runways was complete. The chairman of Wimpey, Sir

Godfrey Mitchell, was a fellow Australian.

The Air Vice-Marshal now needed the approval of the Ministry. On 20 October he wrote to the Director General of Civil Aviation, asking if BSAA could use Heathrow, pointing out that his was a small airline, initially mounting only a tiny operation.

'If we were permitted to use Heathrow we would in the initial stages accept the difficulties of maintenance in the open and would, I am sure, cause no interference with the work of the contractors on the other runways . . .'

A meeting was held in the Deputy Head of Civil Aviation's room at 11 a.m. on 5 December, to discuss Bennett's proposal. It was agreed that BSAA could use Heathrow from 1 January 1946, provided that their operations were described as route-proving flights. This, presumably, was to head off accusations of favouritism from BOAC. A week later the Director General wrote to Bennett, confirming the agreement, and asking that there should be no publicity. The no publicity request was later cancelled by the Minister. Winster was turning out to be an unashamed supporter of Heathrow with a taste for PR.

Bennett himself flew his company's first airliner from the Avro factory near Manchester to Heathrow on 6 December. The brand new aeroplane, registration G-AGWG and named Starlight, was a Lancastrian, an adaptation of the Lancaster bomber design. Bennett's log shows that he touched down at 13.45.

As planned, Heathrow passed from military control to the Ministry of Civil Aviation on 1 January 1946. Don Bennett, always keen to get on with things, arranged for the first flight of British South American to take place on this first day of the new airport. The Minister of Civil Aviation didn't fail to milk maximum publicity from the occasion. Coaches bearing press and dignitaries arrived mid-morning, and drove the 3,000 yard length of the one completed runway. The visitors saw the second runway, 2,000 yards long but only 80 per cent complete, and the third runway, also to be 2,000 yards but a mere 25 per cent finished. They were shown the concrete mixing plant and the concrete spreading machinery on Runway 3. The coaches drove down what was left of Heathrow Lane to see one of the gravel pits still being filled in, then everyone was taken back to the control tower to watch the BSAA departure.

First, Lord Winster inspected Starlight. Don Bennett took him through the passenger cabin, which was only two seats wide, with a centre aisle. There was an onboard toilet. The aeroplane was reckoned to be unusually luxurious, although the spar – the structure which secured the wings to each other – passed right through the cabin and had to be clambered over.

Before take-off Winster made a speech in front of the assembled press, newsfilm crews, dignitaries and members of the public. He boasted about the speed with which the airport was being built, and the speed with which British South American was being enabled to get off the ground. He told the passengers and crew of Starlight that they were about to take off from the finest runway in the world. He declared that Heathrow was a triumph for Britain which would enable us 'to assume our rightful place in the air'.

A full complement of ten passengers queued good naturedly to climb the aircraft steps, duck through the little doorway and enter the cabin. Stewardess Mary Guthrie welcomed them aboard. A former war-time transport pilot, she was the first of Bennett's cabin crew, though not the most senior. Bennett called them Stargirls, just as his airliners were called Starlight, Stardust, and so on.

The four powerful bomber engines were started, and the aeroplane taxied away from the crowd. Besides Bennett, there was on board a crew of two pilots, both former Wing commanders, a flight engineer, a radio operator, an extra radio operator who had come along to learn the route, and Mary Guthrie. From Bennett's point of view the most important thing aboard was 5,000 lbs of the best-paying cargo – mail.

It was a damp day and Runway 1 glistened as Starlight commenced the take-off run, her three-bladed propellers sending back a cloud of spray. The Air Vice-Marshal himself had control of the aircraft, and as she lifted off at 12.05 p.m. he felt elated that his new airline was on its way.

While the VIP party on the ground dug into a buffet lunch laid on in the main workmen's camp, Bennett pointed Starlight towards Lisbon, on the first leg of the long flight to South America. He made the Portuguese capital in 5 hours and 21 minutes, and reached Rio in 28 hours flying time, via Bathurst and Natal. Along the way Bennett had numerous arrangements to make for the appointment of agents for the airline, and in Brazil, Uruguay, and Argentina he negotiated bilateral civil aviation agreements on behalf of the British Government. Local ambassadors helped, but Bennett was the star, the war hero whom the South Americans wished to be associated with.

After the war, South American economies were relatively strong, and there was a big demand for air transport to and from the continent. By March BSAA were flying there twice a week.

On 13 March Lord Winster announced in the House of Lords that Heston Airport would close. With Heathrow poised to become a major airport, Heston was too close to be safe. It was not much more than a mile from the end of Heathrow's Runway No. 1, and Fairey Aviation found themselves moved on once again, this time to White Waltham near Maidenhead.

Towards the end of the month Winster presided at an air display at Heathrow for members of both houses of Parliament, and for air attachés of allied and neutral countries. They were shown several planes, and they took turns to go up in an Avro York. No. 1 Runway was still the only one completed, and some of the ponds were still being drained and filled in. Construction of the other two runways and taxiways was generating a great deal of mud, and, with Wimpey's lorries ceaselessly criss-crossing the site, some mud inevitably found its way on to the operational runway. Winster proudly informed his guests that this untidy building site would eventually be the first experience of Britain for thousands of foreigners. He therefore attached great import-ance to the airport buildings which, he assured them, would be the finest in the country. Winster proclaimed that since the word Heathrow was difficult to pronounce for many foreigners, the place would from now on be known as 'London Airport'.

During these months Hurn, in Dorset, served as the main long-haul land plane terminal for Great Britain, although the airlines which used it were far from happy. They hated having to use an airfield a hundred miles from the capital, and the Ameri-can operators in particular were anxious to find somewhere closer. Passengers disembarking from a transatlantic flight then faced a gruelling three-hour bus ride through the countryside before reaching the comfort of their London hotels. The last leg of this journey brought them along the A30 and on to the Great South West Road, from which indignant passengers could see the new London Airport.

Lord Winster had intended to keep big operators out of Heath-row until the first triangle of runways was complete, but, bowing to pressure, he announced in the Lords that the new airport would officially open on the last day of May. The operators were aware of the almost total lack of passenger facilities but insisted that proximity to London outweighed other considerations. They were happy to accept things as they found them. Some felt that the very fact of having moved there would speed up the building at Heathrow and inject urgency to official procedures and com-mittee meetings.

The first BOAC departure from Heathrow was actually made a few days before the official opening date, by a Lancastrian bound for Australia with six passengers and three bunk beds.

On opening day itself the first plane to touch down was a similar BOAC plane arriving from Australia, lumbering round from Sydney in 63 hours – two hours ahead of schedule.

At noon the Americans arrived from New York. Not one, but two ultra-modern Lockheed Constellations touched down one after the other. Pan American first, then American Overseas Airways. Constellations were the first airliners to have pressurized cabins, enabling them to fly above the weather, increasing speed and bringing air travel into a new era of safety and comfort. Each one could carry fifty passengers, five times as many as the British Lancastrians. On the apron the Constellations gleamed elegantly, in marked contrast to the unmistakably bomber-shaped BOAC machines.

The actual passenger terminal for London Airport occupied an area on the north side, squeezed in between Bath Road and the apron next to Runway 1. It consisted of tents, caravans, a few huts and a row of telephone boxes! The twelve or so tents each had a floor area of 50' by 20', but required a pitching space of 76' by 60'. They were rough and ready, ex-military affairs, made of brown canvas. Departures were organized from one of these tents, and the conditions caused some surprise amongst passengers, particularly the Americans. There were a few comfortable armchairs, oil heaters, and coconut matting on the ground. Check-in staff sat at tables down one side of the tent. There was a W.H.Smith bookstall, a Cable & Wireless desk, a bar, and several cheerful vases of flowers.

In the summer of 1946 it rained almost every day, and duckboards were put down outside, to keep passengers' feet out of the ubiquitous mud. The duckboards also served to keep the passengers away from the treacherous labyrinth of guy ropes which surrounded the tents. Innumerable rows of fire buckets stood ready in case the oil heaters set the tents alight. A couple of 14' by 14' huts housed Elsan toilets. Of the twenty military caravans, half were given to the American operators, and one was used by Special Branch.

To the west of this untidy conglomeration was the control tower, built next to the few yards that were left of Heathrow Road. Of standard RAF design, its solid brickwork towered three storeys over the caravans and canvas. On the ground beside it was a weather station, and to this day meteorological readings are taken at this spot, although the control tower has long disappeared.

The sign at the entrance to the airport read 'London Airport, Heath Row'. The village of Heathrow had occasionally appeared as two words before, on maps and documents over the centuries, but usually it had been spelt as one word. Later signs at London Airport reverted to this form.

In September, work on the triangle of runways was completed, and all three were declared serviceable from 1100 hours on Thursday 19 September. The runway destined to be used the most was the one already in use – Number 1 – because it was aligned with the prevailing westerly wind. Runway 3 was to be temporarily used for aircraft parking. It was agreed that, should the wind change so that this runway was needed, at least one hour's notice would be given, to allow the airlines to move their parked machines elsewhere.

In January 1947 the report of the London Airport Advisory Layout Panel was published, fifteen months after the Panel had been appointed. It was a momentous yet surprisingly thin document of a few pages with accompanying diagrams. The Panel had been asked to identify the best way to build a major airport using as much as they could of the existing runways, which had been designed for RAF needs. They were asked to draw up proposals for a seven-square-mile area which, besides the existing airfield, included a large area to the north of Bath Road as well. The brief specified that this area to the north should not be developed for the first few years, because it included the village of Sipson. The Government preferred to postpone the destruction of Sipson, in the light of a severe post-war housing shortage.

The Layout Panel was made up of ten members, their varied qualifications reflecting expertise in aviation, civil engineering, architecture and administration. A civil servant was chairman. During the course of deliberations, two members left the panel to work abroad. The remaining eight lamented in their preface:

'Guidance from experience elsewhere proved difficult to obtain as there is little knowledge of a multiple-runway airport in civil operation.'

There was plenty of theoretical advice from aviation circles. The pros and cons of all possible layouts were debated at length in every aviation office and cockpit, from Ariel House to Hurn. As a result, the recommendations of the Layout Panel contained few ideas which had not been well aired.

Nevertheless, the Panel chose the most bold and exciting of all the possibilities.

They recommended the retention of only two of the three runways embarked upon for the RAF – the third runway would instead be built half a mile further west, making the triangle bigger. A second triangle of parallel runways would then be superimposed on the first, to form a 'Star of David' layout. It was considered essential to have at least six runways so that, whatever the wind direction, a runway with minimal crosswind could nearly always be found for the delicate business of landing. The advantage of arranging runways in parallel pairs is a doubling of runway capacity. It allows two runways to be used at the same time – usually one for take-offs and one for landing – without much risk of arriving and departing aeroplanes ever getting on a collision course.

Right in the middle of their Star of David the Layout Panel

daringly and imaginatively recommended the siting of the terminal buildings. They were to be reached, dramatically, by a road
tunnel beneath one of the runways.

The proposals thus far the Panel termed 'Stage 2', for which
they suggested a completion date of 1949. What they called 'Stage
1' was the already complete RAF triangle. The third and final
stage was the development north of Bath Road, which the Panel
wanted finished by 1953. Here they envisaged a smaller third
triangle of runways, giving Heathrow an unprecedented three
sets of three parallel runways. Stage 3 would necessitate the
closing of Bath Road. Traffic would be diverted to the north, on to
a new road along the line of Cherry Lane.

The plans made provision for enlarging Heathrow's six principal runways still further, should future aircraft demand it.
Space was left for them to be widened to an astonishing 400 feet!

A word about runway names. The Layout Panel maintained
the numerical titles of the existing runways Numbers 1 and 2,
while the second triangle they dubbed 4, 5 and 7. Number 6 was
the replacement for the third RAF strip, Number 3, which now
disappeared. Numbers 8, 9 and 10 were intended to make up the
separate triangle on the other side of Bath Road. However, air-
crew normally specify runways by a different system, based on
compass bearing. This gives two names to each runway, one for
each direction. For example, Number 1 runway at Heathrow is on
a heading close to 94° when approached from the west, 274° from
the east. The final digit of these numbers is rounded up or down to
the nearest zero (90 and 270), and that zero knocked off (9 and
27). With a parallel pair it must be specified whether the runway
is the one on the left or the right. So Heathrow's oldest runway
when approached from the west is called Runway Zero Nine Left.
From the east the same runway become Two Seven Right.

Considering the small number of aircraft movements in the
early years, accidents at London Airport occurred at an alarming

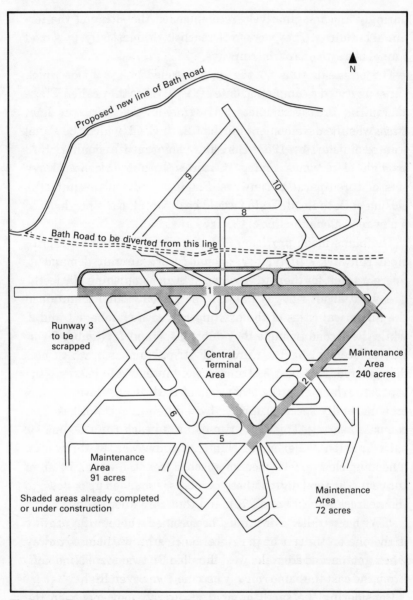

The Layout Panel proposals of 1947. The areas shaded are already completed or under construction

rate. On 19 November 1946, an Anson crash-landed, with the Parliamentary Secretary to the Ministry of Civil Aviation among the passengers. Eight days later, a violent gust of wind blew a Dakota off a taxiway. Nobody was hurt in either of these incidents, but on Friday 25 July 1947 an aircraft experienced brake failure on landing. It careered off the end of the runway, and ran on to the grass. Four passengers were hurt, including the Minister for Overseas Trade, returning from talks in Moscow. The Minister, who was thrown from his seat and injured his ribs, was Harold Wilson.

1947 saw the appointment of the first Commandant of London Airport, Air Marshal Sir John Henry D'Albiac, KCVO, KBE, CB, DSO, a highly likeable fellow with a distinguished war record. In 1940, commanding British forces in Greece, D'Albiac faced 800 German and more than 300 Italian aircraft, with only 80 aircraft on his side. Ceylon in the spring of 1942 was no picnic either. Here a carrier-born attack by the Japanese was beaten off by hacking landing strips out of the jungle. At Heathrow, D'Albiac's military and rather autocratic way of running things was not appreciated by all the airlines. He wanted everything done in the service way, and he showed little understanding of the whims of civilian passengers. But he was recognized as a fine man who did a lot to get things moving along at the new airport. Many remember him for his shooting activities amongst the runways. With friends and colleagues, he would regularly bag pheasant, partridge and hare, all of which were abundant on the airfield. In the evenings, when D'Albiac entertained at his official residence in Longford, he sometimes displayed his talent as a pianist.

The former residents of Heathrow faced a distressing sight if they looked through the perimeter fence towards their old homes. Many of them had welcomed the chance to move into nearby council houses, which were bigger and more comfortable than their Heathrow cottages, but still the loss was felt. Not only their village had been removed, but the entire geography of the district as well. Roads, trees, hedgerows, the lovely ponds, all had been wiped away. On the Bath Road, the start of Heathrow Road was still at the side of 'The Magpies', but after 100 yards it was blocked by a prefabricated hut next to the control tower. Skirting around this, a barrier prevented further progress, but allowed a clear view of the vast flat nothingness.

The Duke of Northumberland's River lay in the path of two of the runways, so it was diverted around the south of the airfield. Its new channel was put alongside Longford River, which was straightened out. Interestingly, the old course of the Duke's River across the airfield can still be seen on modern maps. The river formed the boundary between Harmondsworth and the neighbouring parish, but when the river moved, the boundary stayed. Today that boundary marks the edge of Greater London, and a detailed map will confirm that most of the airport is in Greater London, but the Cargo Terminal, the western extremity of the southern runway and half of Terminal 4 are all in Middlesex.

One landmark was spared. The old hangar from the Great West Aerodrome was used as the fire station for the new airfield. That hangar must have seemed mocking to the Heathrow people, as it stood out there in the middle of the void. Their worst anxieties about Fairey's aerodrome had been realized. Not only had it come to dominate their lives, it had taken their homes.

The new airport and its traffic caught the imagination of larger sections of the British public, and a 350-foot spectator enclosure was provided. Sometimes aeroplanes were parked actually inside the enclosure, purely to give enthusiasts a close look. There were donkey rides to keep the kids happy, and these attracted local families to the airport. But the main attractions were the comings and goings of aircraft, and, one Sunday afternoon in June 1947, 7,000 people paid threepence each to watch them, with a running commentary relayed by loudspeaker.

*

At 8 p.m. on 2 March 1948, a thick fog enveloped London Airport as a Dakota of the Belgian airline Sabena took off from Brussels. Approaching Heathrow, 28-year-old pilot Henri Goblet was told that visibility on the ground was down to twenty yards. Goblet made the decision to land. Soon after 9 p.m he was on final approach, being 'talked down' by controllers in the tower, when he nose-dived into the ground, fifty yards from the runway. There was an explosion, followed by a fierce fire. Three survivors were rescued before the heat became too intense. After an hour the fire had burned itself out, and there was nothing to show that the remains had been an aeroplane, except for one wing tilted towards the sky. By the early hours of the morning all nineteen bodies had been recovered. It was the worst accident to have happened at Heathrow.

The Boeing company on the west coast of the United States thrilled the world by producing the first ever double-decker land plane. The Stratocruiser had an onboard staircase which led down to a cocktail bar on a lower deck. Pan American took delivery of the first production model, put her on the prestigious New York–London route, and in June 1949 she touched down at Heathrow for the first time.

It wasn't until six months later that the first Stratocruiser service of BOAC took off from Heathrow. The British carrier had hoped to have Sir Winston Churchill aboard for this important flight to New York. They were six months behind the Americans with a new plane on a vital route, and they wanted a publicity coup to make up for lost time. When Churchill was unable to oblige, Sir John D'Albiac agreed to take his place, together with a real British bulldog. The canine passenger was intended to catch the attention of newspaper picture editors. As it was the dog was sick all the way, the plane arrived in New York a day late, and Lady D'Albiac's luggage was found to be full of water.

The problems were soon ironed out, and Stratocruisers went on to establish themselves as firm favourites with passengers and crews alike. Their success was the final nail in the coffin of flying boats, which had previously been the only double-decker aeroplanes available. Now even that feature, and the spaciousness that went with it, had been copied by a land aeroplane. Flying boats had lost one of their few advantages over land planes, and with that they began their final disappearance from the airline fleets of the world.

Apart from BOAC, which by now had swallowed BSAA, the other great post-war British carrier was British European Airways. Formed in 1946 from a division of BOAC, BEA was given routes served until then by RAF Transport Command. While BOAC provided long-haul services, BEA's role was to serve destinations in the United Kingdom and the rest of Europe. The London terminal for BEA was RAF Northolt, six miles to the north of Heathrow. This military field was still open to civil airlines, but notice was given that the RAF wanted to resume sole use by 1954. BEA gradually began to transfer their services to the giant new airfield to the south, and their first scheduled departure from Heathrow was a Paris-bound Viking on 16 April 1950.

Early one evening in October of that year, a similar aircraft was returning from Paris. This particular BEA Viking was expected at Northolt but, because of fog, was diverted to Heathrow, where the runways were longer and wider, the safety facilities more elaborate. Just before 8 o'clock the pilot established himself on the ILS, and began to follow the radio beam down to the runway. By now visibility on the ground was classified '40 yards', and it was decided that this would have to be the last plane allowed to land. As anxious controllers waited in the mist-shrouded tower, the airliner came down, struck the concrete at the intersection of Runways 1 and 3, bounced, and hit a pile of iron drainpipes 500 yards off the runway. There was a flash so bright that it was visible at the control tower through the thick fog. A stewardess and one man were thrown clear. As the aircraft caught fire, nine fire-engines and five ambulances raced around in the fog, unable to locate the stricken airliner. When they did find her, they were unable to see what they were doing, and anyway the intense heat kept them back. At 10 p.m. the fog lifted and the wreckage was revealed, still smouldering. It was the worst crash at Heathrow so far, with twenty-eight killed.

Always the building work went on. The tents lasted until the autumn of 1946, and were replaced by prefabricated one-storey buildings of concrete frame and fibreboard, and later by a two-storey concrete structure. The recommendations of the Layout Panel had been largely accepted by the Civil Aviation Ministry, and work was well advanced on Stage 2. Runway 5, parallel with Number 1 was now open. From 1950, Number 1 had to be temporarily closed, when a huge ditch was dug across it. In this great ditch, a concrete tunnel was being built, to take four lanes of road traffic beneath the runway. 2,080 feet long and 86 feet wide, it was to link the outside world with the inside of the Star of David, the 'Central Area' where passenger terminals would be built. The newly appointed architect was already hard at work. In his late thirties, Frederick Gibberd was a graduate of Birmingham School of Architecture who had earned a solid reputation designing housing schemes. His successes at Heathrow were later to be crowned by his famous masterpiece – the Roman Catholic Cathedral at Liverpool.

On 1 February 1952, King George VI and the Queen came to London Airport to bid farewell to their daughter, Princess Elizabeth, and the Duke of Edinburgh, who were leaving for a five-month tour of the Commonwealth. Thousands crowded the roadside and the public enclosure. The King was especially warmly cheered – this was the first time he had been seen since his recent illness. The Duke and Duchess of Gloucester, the Mountbattens, the Churchills and Princess Margaret all went inside the young couple's Argonaut airliner, together with the King and Queen. The High Commissioners of Australia, New Zealand and Ceylon also paid their respects.

After ten minutes Churchill left the aircraft, followed by the others. The King and Queen watched from the apron as the Argonaut's engines started up, then they retired to the roof of the adjacent VIP lounge. The royal aircraft taxied to the distant Runway 5. With the Central Area under construction, piles of gravel obscured the view as the departing aircraft accelerated in a westerly direction, lifting off at 12.11 p.m., first stop El Adem in Libya. Accompanied by Sir John D'Albiac and the Chairman of BOAC, the King stood bare headed in a heavy coat, watching the aeroplane until it was just a speck against the grey clouds.

That was the last time the King saw his daughter, for a week later he suffered a fatal coronary thrombosis. Princess Elizabeth now became Queen, and she and the Duke of Edinburgh immediately flew home from Entebbe. On the 7 February they landed at Heathrow at 4.19 in the afternoon. The Duke of Gloucester, Churchill and the Mountbattens were waiting to meet them and escort them to Clarence House. The royal aircraft rolled towards the reception party on the apron, and came to a halt at 4.30. The young Queen Elizabeth II emerged, descended the aircraft steps, and for the first time set foot in her new kingdom.

Post-war aviation was dominated by American aircraft. The Douglas Dakota had proved to be the most popular airliner ever, and the innovative Constellations and Stratocruisers had maintained the American lead. Suddenly Great Britain took the initiative by harnessing the jet engine for passengers. Throughout the history of aviation, innovations in fighter design had a few years later been applied to civil aircraft. But somehow the jet engine had seemed too explosive a form of propulsion to follow this pattern, until the de Havilland company announced plans for a jet-propelled transatlantic mail carrier. This original brief was modified until the DH type 106 emerged, a four-engined jet with thirty-six seats and a 500 m.p.h. top speed which was 25 per cent faster than the latest Constellation. De Havilland named their revolutionary aeroplane The Comet.

BOAC took delivery of the first production Comet on the last day of 1951, and four months later they put fare-paying passengers aboard for the first time, on their route to Johannesburg via Rome, Beirut, Khartoum, Entebbe and Livingstone.

The full load of thirty-six passengers arrived from the airline's Victoria terminal forty-five minutes before take-off. It was a warm and sunny spring afternoon. Sir Geoffrey de Havilland and his chief designer were at the airport, and large crowds filled the public enclosure, and lined balconies and roofs. All eyes were on the shiny skin and sleek shape of the airliner without propellers. As the engines were started up, an ear-piercing scream filled the air, giving the crowd a foretaste of the ghastly environmental cost of jet travel. As the airliner moved off for the long taxi down to Runway 5, the awful scream lessened slightly. At 3.12 there was a thunderous roar, the Comet shot along the runway, pointed itself towards the sky at what seemed an impossible angle, and lifted off. The world's first commercial jet flight for passengers was under way.

The arrival of jets brought many complications, but at least with them there were no accidents involving people walking into moving propellers. Such tragedies happened most frequently at night, in the dazzle of electric lights. Pure jets, however, did bring with them the hazards of 'jet blast', the very rapidly moving column of air expelled from the back of a jet engine. The air, pungent with exhaust gases, moved rapidly enough to kill grass, and to add significantly to the wear and tear on runways. Jet blast could pick up stones and hurl them at whatever might be behind the aircraft, which sometimes included windows or people.

In front of buildings, fence-like blast deflectors became indispensible, as they directed the blast harmlessly upwards, and stopped the stones. Top engineer Alastair Macrae was faced with a surprising problem caused by jets. Along the sides of the runways at Heathrow, manhole lids protected subterranean electrical junction boxes. These lids were heavy concrete affairs, but still Macrae had to have them modified when he discovered to his amazement that jet blast was lifting them up.

The plans to extend the airfield to the other side of Bath Road aroused controversy. Many opposed the scheme entirely, saying London Airport was quite big enough already. In aviation circles there was criticism of the Layout Panel idea to use the extension for a third triangle of runways. It was asked whether some other layout might not be more useful. A pair of short runways converging at about 150° was suggested, for light aircraft. Others argued for one huge runway, on the 10/28 alignment. This would give a total of three really big parallel runways in the direction of the prevailing wind, increasing the number of aircraft that could be handled. This, it was argued, would make London Airport indisputably the best in the world.

The intention to extend was affecting the area badly. The village of Sipson was expected to be demolished completely, and the place took on an air of gloom and doom. Buildings and land were allowed to run down in anticipation of the destruction. The people of nearby Harlington and Harmondsworth dreaded finding themselves under the flight path to a new runway.

In December 1952 the Conservative Minister of Civil Aviation, Alan Lennox-Boyd, replying in the Commons to a question from the local MP, Freddie Beswick (Uxbridge, Labour), announced that the extension would not be carried out after all. With a Parliamentary brevity he explained:

'Careful analysis of the results of a programme of practical experiments recently concluded by my department have shown that the additional amount of traffic which could be accepted by extending the airport north of the Bath Road would not justify the expenditure and disturbance caused by the extension.'

There was much rejoicing in Sipson. Two schools, a church and several hundred houses had been saved from the bulldozer.

By the end of 1953 the tunnel was open, and contractors' vehicles were able to reach the building site in the Central Area without crossing Runway 1.

The number of passengers passing through the airport was still growing fast, and in 1953 the total exceeded a million for the first time.

The Comet, meanwhile, was enjoying its position as world leader in airliner design. No self-respecting airline could now afford to be without jet speed and comfort, and more and more of the wonder machines were being seen and heard at London Airport. The future was looking rosy for de Havilland and Great Britain. However there was one doubt about the plane.

Earlier in the year, a BOAC Comet was making its customary steep climb after take-off from Dum Dum Airport at Calcutta, when it suddenly crashed to earth, killing everybody aboard. The disaster happened in a severe tropical storm, and puzzled experts could find no explantion other than the weather. A Court of Enquiry eventually blamed structural failure causing fire, but there was no detailed explanation.

The following January another BOAC Comet left Rome on the last leg of its run from Singapore to Heathrow. There were six crew and twenty-nine passengers aboard, ten of them children. Twenty minutes after take-off the airliner was still climbing when the pilot made what was to be his last report, saying he was on course, and mentioning nothing out of the ordinary. Minutes later, between the islands of Elba and Monte Cristo, the airliner broke up in mid-air. Local fisherman Giovanni di Marco later told the press:

'I was fishing just south of the island when I heard the whine of the plane above me. It was above the clouds. I could not see it. Then I heard three explosions, very quickly, one after the other. For a moment all was quiet. Then, several miles away, I saw a silver thing flash out of the clouds. Smoke came from it. It hit the sea. There was a great cloud of water. By the time I got there, all was still again. There were some bodies in the water. We began to pick them up. There was nothing else we could do.'

Giovanni and his friends brought fifteen bodies to the local harbour, where they were laid out on planks at the quayside. A priest imparted benedictions.

All BOAC Comets were immediately grounded, and at Heathrow a crisis meeting was held to decide what to do about the planes. Representatives of airlines, manufacturers, the Air Registration Board and the Accidents Investigation Branch could find little to indicate the cause of this second Comet crash. Weeks of examination revealed nothing either, so fifty modifications were made in the vague hope that one of them would remove the cause of the crash. On 23 March, Comet services were allowed to resume.

Only a fortnight later, a third Comet failed to return to London Airport. The world was stunned. The Calcutta crash could be blamed on freak weather. The Elba disaster might have been a bomb. But now there was a third crash, and all three were in similar circumstances, as the aircraft was climbing to her high cruising altitude, minutes after take-off. Surely there must be something wrong with the aeroplane.

This latest tragedy happened after take-off from Rome, this time crashing into very deep water off the coast of Sicily. All that was to be seen of the airliner and her fourteen passengers was the limited amount of wreckage buoyant enough to float to the surface, and a patch of oil ¼ mile by ¾ mile.

The Comet's Certificate of Airworthiness was immediately

withdrawn pending investigations, and the Royal Navy was asked to make renewed efforts to recover the wreckage of the earlier Elba crash, which was lying at a shallower depth.   In the autumn of 1954, a Court of Enquiry lasting five weeks concluded that all three crashes had been caused by the same weakness in the fuselage. Repeated cycles of extreme pressurization necess-itated by the high cruising altitude of the plane had caused great stress and, eventually, metal fatigue. The design fault was so difficult to put right that the Comet appeared doomed. De Havil-land persisted, however, and eventually a perfectly safe successor did emerge, bringing the company a deserved commercial reward.

BOAC, in the meantime, found themselves with 20 per cent of their capacity grounded. They had no choice but to order more Stratocruisers and Constellations from America. The sound of jets would not be heard at Heathrow, or any other airport, for many years.

In 1954 the Royal Aeronautical Society held another summer garden party at Heathrow, their first since the pre-war gather-ings at the Fairey field. How things had changed from those days! Now the event was held in the middle of hundreds of acres of concrete at a major international airport, with displays having to fit in with the scheduled arrivals and departures of the world's airlines. Parked for inspection were a Stratocruiser, a Super Constellation and a Viscount, the exciting new turbo-prop from the British Vickers company. The Fairey Aviation Works Band played in the background. The event, though, did not seem at home at the new Heathrow. It was held at the southern tip of the unfinished Central Area, squeezed in by the still incomplete terminal building. Yet again at this event the weather was unkind, and everyone went home soaked to the skin and lashed by the wind. This turned out to be the last RAeS garden party.

A few days later, on the thirty-fifth anniversary of Alcock and Brown's historic first non-stop Atlantic flight, the Minister of

Transport and Civil Aviation unveiled a statue of the pioneering duo, at the edge of the apron next to the old terminal buildings. It's a popular work, with the brave young aviators captured in stone, complete with flying overalls and goggles. It now stands in the Central Area, on the west side of the control tower.

At the end of 1954, the RAF loan of Northolt for civil aviation came to an end. BEA and many European operators relunctantly transferred their operations to Heathrow, more than doubling the traffic there. Passenger facilities were stretched almost to bursting, and conditions for the travelling public were not what the airlines would have liked. However, they looked forward to the opening of the Central Area terminal, promised within a few months.

BEA brought with them to Heathrow their Viscounts, the speedy, fuel-efficient, short-range turbo-props which were, since the grounding of the Comets, the showpiece of British plane-making. Within months of the airline's arrival, one of these new aircraft was in an accident which may have been caused partly by the pilot being unfamiliar with his new base. The aircraft was bound for Istanbul via Rome and Athens, with five crew and twenty-five passengers. The captain was instructed by Ground Control to taxi westwards along Number 1 runway, and then turn left on to Number 6 for take-off. The aircraft was leaving in poor visibility, and unfortunately she turned left too soon, on to the old Number 3. This runway had been closed for the construction of the Central Area, and half-way down its length it became a building site. Unaware of this, the crew of the Viscount pushed the throttles fully forward for take-off. The plane had accelerated to 80 m.p.h. when she struck a steel barrier. The undercarriage collapsed, the port engines were torn out, and the fuel tanks burst open. Fortunately there was no fire, and somehow there were no fatalities or even serious injuries. However, a Feltham ambulance, returning to base after the accident, managed to hit a police car, and two policemen were detained in hospital.

Since 1946 London Airport had been getting busier at an accelerating rate. In its first year of operation the airport handled 60,000 passengers. For 1955/56 that figure was close to 3,000,000.

# 4
# Central Area

In April 1955 the Central Area came into use. This was later than originally intended by the Layout Panel, thanks largely to Government cut-backs, and strikes.

The Central Area was dominated by the 120-foot brick control tower. Ground controllers direct aircraft along runways and taxiways from their position on the top floor, where they enjoy a unique view of the whole airfield through 360° of green-tinted double glazing. Two storeys below, on the sixth floor, the approach controllers pore over their radar screens, and line aircraft up for landing. Lower floors house meteorological and administrative offices, rest and recreation rooms.

On the south-east side of the Central Area was the long-awaited new passenger terminal. Long-haul passengers had to continue using the old Bath Road terminal until 1962. The new terminal, then called 'The Europa Building' but since renamed 'Terminal 2', has remained almost exclusively for short-haul services to Europe and the Mediterranean, with domestic flights operating at first through the sectioned-off 'Britannic' annexe. The Europa was very much a building of its time, modelled like a giant 1950s radiogram.

On the airfield side of the building – the 'air side' – a concrete apron accommodated the parked airliners in two rows. With passengers embarking and disembarking, and various vehicles attending the aircraft, it was felt that the apron was liable to get dangerously busy. For vehicles servicing the furthest row, a tunnel was provided, so that the vehicles wouldn't have to cross the paths of arriving or departing aircraft. However, this tunnel, and similar ones beneath the north-east and south-west aprons (some just for pedestrians) were never used to any great extent. Aeroplanes, lorries and people were able to go about their business reasonably safely without tunnels, it emerged over the years. The disused entrances to two of these tunnels can still be seen today, on either side of the entrance to the main tunnel.

The official opening of the Central Area was performed on 16 December by the Queen. Before the ceremony, Her Majesty had

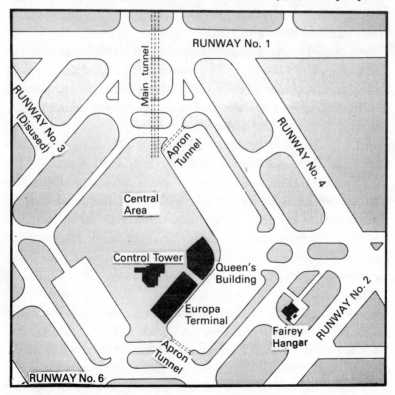

The Central Area, late 1955

told her staff of her special feeling for Heathrow, as it was the place where she first set foot on English soil as Queen. When she arrived and made her tour of inspection, The Queen went largely unnoticed by the stream of passengers rushing for their flights. Wearing an air force blue coat, grey hat, and diamond brooch in the shape of BOAC's Speedbird symbol, Her Majesty unveiled a stone plaque in the third major building of the Central Area. Its name, she revealed, was to be 'The Queen's Building'. This is the pilots' administration and briefing centre for Heathrow, where aircrews report and receive flight plans. The roof boasts an observation area, which has proved popular with enthusiasts and 'weepers and greeters'. Originally The Queen's Building also contained public restaurants and a news cinema.

Her Majesty was accompanied by John Boyd-Carpenter, the Minister responsible for civil aviation, a post now described as Minister of Transport and Civil Aviation. Also in attendance was Sir John D'Albiac and John Profumo, the efficient young Parliamentary Secretary to the Minister.

After tea in the restaurant of The Queen's Building, the Queen crossed to the control tower as dusk approached. Climbing the steps into the ground control room at the top of the tower, Her Majesty was shown a wonderful view of the airfield, revealed all around her. As she entered, the lights of the airfield were switched on. With the predominantly white lights of London beyond, the geometry of the runways and taxiways was painted in with lights of red, white, yellow, green and blue.

On 1 October 1956, an RAF Avro Vulcan jet bomber was approaching Runway 10 Left. The idea was for the big bomber to mark her return to Britain from a 26,000 mile tour of Australia and New Zealand with a grand appearance at Britain's principal airport. Unfortunately the delta-winged jet approached too low, and came down in a cabbage field at the end of the runway. Leaving its wheels amongst the vegetables, the big bomber carried on, caught fire, and deposited itself in pieces along the runway. The only two survivors escaped by ejector seat. They were the pilot and no less a person than Air Marshal Sir Harry Broadhurst, C-in-C Bomber Command, who was acting as second pilot.

After ten years as Commandant, Sir John D'Albiac retired in 1957. He was replaced by Group Captain James Jeffs, a jovial giant of a man who was rarely seen without a Senior Service between his fingers. Jimmy Jeffs' life has been inextricably bound up with the events of the Heathrow story. He once came second to Fairey test pilot Chris Staniland in a motor race at Brooklands. His name was synonymous with Air Traffic Control. He played a part in the early development of ATC when he worked at Croydon in the '20s, and it was he who installed ATC at most of the principal airports of the United Kingdom. When he was in charge of ATC at Heston, he used to supervise the flying shows at the RAeS garden parties. He was at the Great West Aerodrome for the King's secret arrival in September 1936, and he was in the tower at Heston on Chamberlain's return from Munich in September 1938. During the war, Jeffs set up the transatlantic control centre at Prestwick. In 1945 he was put in charge of ATC for the London Division, which included the new Heathrow, and he was present at Don Bennett's historic first scheduled departure. During D'Albiac's time, he sometimes took part in the shooting parties. From 1950 to 1957 Jeffs was Commandant at Prestwick. He served for only three years at Heathrow, but people there grew fond of him in that short time, and the airlines were sorry to see him go.

The continually escalating passenger figures at Heathrow were still causing concern. Something needed to be done to make provision for more and more passengers and planes. What was the best way of using the space available?

To ponder the options, a committee was set up under the chairmanship of Sir Eric Millbourn, the head of a shipping company, and, in August 1957, Sir Eric and his colleagues produced a list of radical recommendations, most of which were acted upon.

First and foremost, they urged the expansion of Gatwick Airport, to take pressure off Heathrow. At Heathrow itself, they endorsed the Layout Panel view that all terminals should be in the Central Area. They recommended the immediate construction of a new long-haul terminal, on the south-west face of the diamond which made up the Central Area. On the north-east face, the committee wanted a new short-haul terminal just for BEA, and on the last face of the diamond, the north-west, they suggested a terminal for cargo.

The Millbourn Committee also advocated the 'finger and gate' system. Instead of passengers walking across the apron or being driven by bus to reach their aeroplanes, this system has them walking through a covered walkway - the finger. Along the length of the finger are a series of doors - the gates - leading to steps down to the apron. There is a gate for each aircraft stand. The aeroplanes park with their noses up to the finger and, before they can be on their way, have to be pushed back by a special tractor called an air tug. The fingers in this system are sometimes called 'piers'. The finger and gate system brought new standards of comfort, and soon led to the development of loading bridges – the flexible corridors that connect directly with the aircraft door.

With the Millbourn Committee calling for so much building, there was clearly going to be a problem fitting everything into the limited space of the Central Area. To enable the Central Area to expand slightly, the committee reluctantly recommended the closure of two of the airport's six runways, namely the parallel pair 4 and 6, aligned in the little-used north-west to south-east direction.

The long-haul terminal was embarked upon without delay. Frederick Gibberd produced a design that was an updated version of his earlier Europa Terminal. It was larger and more airy, with less brick and more glass. Its exact position somewhat destroyed the symmetry of the Central Area, as it was built well to the west, to leave room for car parking. It was named the Oceanic Terminal (later renamed Terminal 3), and on 16 November 1961 BOAC moved in. In March 1962, the other long-haul carriers followed, leaving the old Bath Road terminal to be used for cargo only. At last all passenger operations were in the Central Area, as planned by the Layout Panel fifteen years before.

Heathrow now entered a special phase in its history, when the drive through the tunnel gave the Central Area a special atmosphere. All passenger journeys started and ended here. The bold concept of terminals in the midst of runways was to prove more and more restrictive as the years passed, but it did produce a dense 'airport city' of concentrated excitement, a glamorous enclave of global travel isolated from the workaday world.

The Oceanic Terminal was put up close to a site already taken by the oil companies on a long lease. Here aviation fuel, which smells and behaves a lot like paraffin, is decanted into tanker lorries (known in the industry as 'bowsers') for distribution to aircraft. It amazes passengers to this day that such an inflammable operation is still carried out within a cigarette throw of the car park.

In 1962 The Beatles began their rise to world fame, and their comings and goings through Heathrow came to be regularly documented by press and TV. On one occasion drummer Ringo Starr was persuaded to hold a sign reading TLES up to the BEA logo on the plane he was boarding, resulting in a publicity coup for both airline and group. Another time, nearly 10,000 teenagers spent the night in The Queen's Building before giving their idols a screaming farewell the following day. The popularity of The Beatles was never surpassed and, although The Monkees and Michael Jackson attracted big crowds to the airport, these were not on the scale of Beatlemania.

The painfully slow drive between Heathrow and central London was speeded up in 1965, with the opening of a new section of the M4. This motorway starts its journey from Chiswick balanced on concrete posts above the Great West Road, before leaving the line of the old road to climb over a factory, descending back to the ground in hitherto tranquil Osterley Park. The motorway cuts right through the middle of former Heston Airport, where the westbound service area is built in front of the old hangars, now part of an industrial estate. I wonder how many passengers taking the road to Heathrow realize that they are driving through what nearly became London's main airport.

A branch from the main motorway brought traffic speeding right to the airport boundary. This M4 spur approached in a cutting, passed beneath the Bath Road, and came right to the tunnel entrance. Journey times were reduced still further, and passengers arriving in Britain were given a first impression of a modern nation with efficient transport. The old entrance from Bath Road became very much the side door.

In October 1965 tragedy struck again when a BEA Vanguard returning from Edinburgh attempted to land in fog. Another Vanguard had successfully touched down half an hour before, and the crew were being 'talked down' by the radar controllers in the tower. At the last moment the airliner tried to overshoot but it was too late. It hit the runway and exploded in a mass of flames. All thirty-six aboard perished, including a baby, making this Heathrow's worst disaster.

Up until this time, London Airport had been operating against a background of some discontent. The airlines spoke of bureaucratic inefficiency and remote control of the airport by civil servants in Whitehall. The London airports as as whole were losing money. As early as 1961, a Select Committee of the House of Commons issued a shatteringly critical report on the situation, reviving the idea that an independent authority should be established to manage

Looking north-east over the Great West Aerodrome in 1935. A garden party is in progress, including what looks like a fire-fighting display. The single hangar, with the owner's name 'Fairey' painted on the roof, is beyond the aeroplanes lined up for inspection. All the land in this photograph is today part of the airfield.

1 January 1946. Formalities before the first passenger-carrying flight from Heathrow. The Minister of Civil Aviation delivers a speech beneath 'Starlight', a Lancastrian of British South American Airways bound for Buenos Aires. On the Minister's left, holding a briefcase, is the chairman of BSAA, Air Vice-Marshal Don Bennett, who, on this flight, captained the plane himself.

Heathrow, Summer 1946. The terminal area of London Airport, where passengers checked in and waited for their flights in a brown ex-military tent. Bath Road runs in front of the houses in the background. The apron is to the right, out of shot. The destinations served from here were those beyond Europe.

A Dakota DC-3 on the taxiway in front of the original RAF control tower in 1952.

Terminal 3 as it appeared when first opened in 1961. This façade by Frederick Gibberd was replaced by a high-tech blue skin when the building was enlarged and remodelled in the late 1980s.

Looking south at the passenger tunnel under construction by Taylor Woodrow in about 1952. In the foreground, the airfield's northernmost taxiway remains uninterrupted for the time being. Further away, the main runway is very definitely interrupted by the work. Beyond, another taxiway is relaid over a completed section of tunnel. In the distance, a dark pile of building material lies on the closed Runway 3.

Looking north-west over the Central Area around 1964. On the left, the first multi-storey car park is open. Foreground: Europa Building, later Terminal 2. Right: The Queen's Building. The area of parked cars beyond the Queen's Building is today occupied by Terminal 1.

The 1968 707 disaster. The BOAC jet has just landed with its wing ablaze. Moments later the whole plane was engulfed in the flames. This previously unpublished photo was taken by quick-witted amateur photographer Doris Follows.

The stricken BOAC 707 burns on Runway 05 Right during the disaster of April 1968. The skill of the captain and others restricted the fatalities to five. There have been no disasters on this scale since.

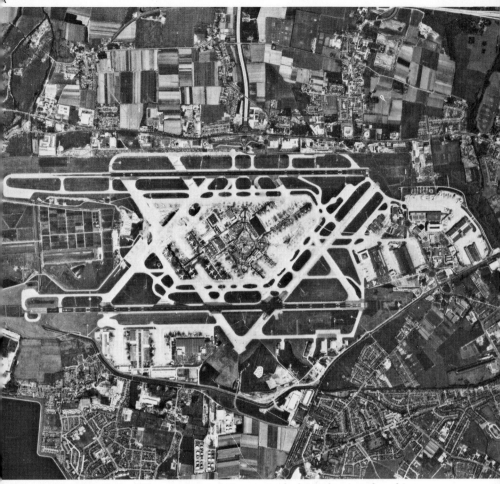

eathrow in the 1970s. Some of the runways are being encroached upon by aircraft parking.
umber 1 and Number 5 have been extended and overslabbed. Around the airport many
ricultural fields have been preserved by planning restrictions.

Looking north-west along Cain's Lane in 1987. Today this former rural byway is closed off at the airfield perimeter. It used to continue in a straight line for a mile, into the village of Heathrow, where the terminals of the Central Area now stand.

Terminal 4 looking north. The new terminal is separated from the Central Area by two intersecting runways, the busy asphalt-surfaced Number 5, and the less often used Number 2. In the foreground are Duke's River and (nearest) Longford River.

## AIRLIFE PUBLISHING LTD.

Thank you for buying this Airlife book. If you would like to be kept informed about our forthcoming publications, please fill in this card.

Name: ................................................................................

Address: ...........................................................................

..........................................................................................

1) In order to assist our editors in determining the type of aviation books our readers require could you please tick your areas of interest in the spaces below.

      Historic Aviation ☐    Books for Pilots ☐    Naval Aviation ☐

Contemporary Aviation ☐    Aero-Modelling ☐    Civil Aviation ☐

2) How did this book come to your notice?

☐ Magazine Advertisement. Which magazine? _____

☐ Book Review. Which publication? _____

☐ In a bookshop. Which bookshop? _____

3) In which book did you find this card? _____
(Please specify title)

AIRLIFE PUBLISHING LTD.
101 LONGDEN ROAD
SHREWSBURY
SHROPSHIRE SY3 9BR

the London group of airports. Many drew an analogy between the proposed body and the Port of London Authority. A White Paper suggested that 'an airports authority should be set up to own and manage the main international airports now owned by the state'.

Introducing the Airports Authority Bill in 1965, Labour Minister of Aviation Roy Jenkins enthused that the Authority would be able deal in a more flexible, adaptable and rapid manner with essentially commercial problems. Both sides of the House broadly agreed with him, and the Bill received the Royal Assent on 2 June. The British Airports Authority was the name given to the new body, and it was entrusted with the three London airports of Heathrow, Gatwick and Stansted, as well as Prestwick in Scotland.

The man invited to become the first chairman of the BAA was the Cambridge graduate who had cycled to the Great West Aerodrome in the 1930s to work in the drawing office. Now 51, Peter Masefield had established himself as a major figure in British aviation. A man of great eloquence and charm, he served from 1943 to 1945 as Secretary to the War Cabinet Committee on Post-War Civil Air Transport, followed by two years in charge of long-term planning at the new Civil Aviation Ministry. As Chief Executive of BEA from 1949-55, he turned loss into profit, before moving to manufacture as Managing Director of Bristol Aircraft. Masefield was surprised to be asked to do the BAA job. He knew that the first Chairman would face a unique challenge in aviation, having to turn the airports' bureaucracy into an efficient money-earner. He could think of a lot of things that he would like to see done. He took the job.

The Minister announced that the 'vesting date', when the BAA would take over ownership of the airports, would be 1 April 1966. More appointments were made, offices found in Buckingham Gate next to Buckingham Palace, and hurried preparations made for the hand-over. When the vesting date finally arrived,

Masefield held a press conference and, with his board and senior officers, made a tour of his four airports.

Heathrow's future was now bound up with the three other fields in the group.

Gatwick had become London's second airport, and was expected to take on a bigger role as traffic at Heathrow approached saturation. It still had only one runway, though, and, at twenty-six miles from central London, was shunned by the scheduled airlines. BEA and Air France had both resisted attempts by the Ministry to shift their operations to Gatwick. Despite a direct rail link with Victoria Station in London, the Sussex field continued to be used mainly by charter airlines carrying package holiday customers. The seasonal nature of this trade meant that for a busy July and August Gatwick had to provide facilities which remained largely idle for the remainder of the year. This under-utilization of staff and capital investment meant that Gatwick was running at a loss of half a million pounds a year.

The third of the London airports, Stansted, was a time-consuming thirty-five miles from London, more than twice as far out as Heathrow. Little flying took place here at this time, most of that being concerned with general aviation or training. Stansted's role was seen as lying in the decades ahead.

The fourth airport entrusted to the BAA was Prestwick. Near Ayr on the south-west coast of Scotland, this airfield had been a busy transatlantic staging post during the war, but now languished as a nice airport doomed to be in the wrong place. The population centres of Glasgow and Edinburgh, respectively thirty and sixty miles distant, were just too far away to use it. The future for Prestwick looked precarious.

At Heathrow there was a lucky escape for many in April 1968. A BOAC 707 was making an afternoon departure for Sydney from 28 Left. A few moments after take-off, the Boeing was making a turn to the left when the port inner engine started to play up.

Before the fuel could be shut off one of the lines was severed and the fuel ignited, resulting in an explosion. The three-ton engine broke away and fell into a disused gravel pit near Thorpe, coming to rest under twenty feet of murky green water. Meanwhile the fire had spread to the wing. Captain Charles Taylor wrestled the aircraft back to Heathrow to make a brilliant cross-wind landing on Runway 05 Right, just before the whole wing broke off at the root. Aided by the crew and the emergency shutes, all but five of those on board leapt clear moments before the fuselage became an inferno. Pop singer Mark Wynter, flying to Australia to marry, was among those unhurt.

Fashionable student revolution touched Heathrow in June 1968, when German-born French student leader Daniel Cohn-Bendit arrived to take part in a BBC TV discussion of student unrest. Frightening Paris riots, involving street barricades and petrol bombs, had shaken France, causing Cohn-Bendit to be banned from that country. The immigration authorities at Heathrow took a similar view, and prevented the student leader from entering Britain. A crowd of students were impatiently awaiting the arrival of their hero in the Europa Terminal, and when he failed to appear they staged a demonstration. British student leader Tariq Ali was particularly vocal, and another student leader stood on one of the seats to address surprised passengers, before police broke up the demonstration. After a couple of hours Cohn-Bendit emerged with permission to stay for twenty-four hours. The television debate turned out to be dull and uneventful.

Three weeks later there was another terrible accident, when a propeller aircraft bringing in race horses from Deauville for stud farms in the south of England was making a normal approach to 28 Right. Seconds from touch-down, metal fatigue caused a control rod in a flap of the port wing to fall away suddenly, causing that wing to dip towards the ground. The wing-tip scraped along the runway, causing the freighter to slew to the left as it came down. It careered along the ground towards the Central Area, where two parked Tridents stood in its path. The first one had its tail smashed off, the second was ripped in half, its tailplane and engines coming to rest a hundred feet away. The freighter itself smashed into a metal barrier in front of a building site, landed upside down, and burst into flames. The pitiful sounds of horses in terror were heard from the fire. The crew, three of the five grooms aboard and all eight horses were killed.

This incident, in 1968, was the last major catastrophe within the perimeter of Heathrow Airport.

The airport's first place of worship was dedicated jointly by the Archbishops of Canterbury and Westminster in October. The Anglican and Roman Catholic primates had jointly launched the appeal to raise the £100,000 needed for the new building. It was built away from noise, underground, on the south side of the control tower. A cool, cavernous place, this interdenominational chapel is a marvellous haven of tranquillity and is open throughout every day.

At Stockholm Airport, a new Customs idea had been tried, and was proving both efficient and popular. HM Customs and the BAA decided to try the same thing at Heathrow. Separate Red and Green channels were introduced. Passengers were invited to walk through Green if they were not carrying goods on which duty was payable, or Red if they were. With an ever greater flow of passengers into the country, Customs officers were grateful to be spared the ritual of asking 'Have you anything to declare?'

On 19 December thieves helped themselves to a particularly generous Christmas present. £104,000 worth of diamonds, gold dust and US currency notes, all awaiting shipment to Tokyo, were sitting in a Pan Am strongroom. The thieves cut through the hasp on the doors, and opened two other doors with duplicate keys, moving so quietly that even the guards on the premises were not disturbed. A security patrol at midnight discovered nothing wrong, and the theft was not discovered until 7 a.m.

The amount of cargo passing through the airport was increasing even more dramatically than the number of passengers, and it soon became clear that the Millbourn Committee recommendation of a freight terminal in the Central Area would not be adequate. Instead a site was found along the southern edge of the airfield, bordered by Runway 5 on the one side, and the village of Stanwell on the other.

A tunnel was needed to move cargo to and from passenger planes parked in the Central Area, but by now Heathrow was so busy that Runway 5 could not be taken out of service, so the cut and cover method used to build the passenger tunnel could not be used for the cargo tunnel. Instead, a single thirty-three foot diameter tube was excavated mole-fashion between Runways 5 and 6, a distance of 3,000 feet. The cargo tunnel is not open to the public because it is on the air side, a bonded area, with customs checks between it and the outside world. However, it is possible for anybody to travel through this tunnel by bus, either London Transport or the free inter-terminal shuttle. Naturally the bus does not open its doors within the bonded area.

In December 1968, faults were noticed in the roof of the inbound passenger tunnel. There was a distinct danger of pieces of concrete falling on to the cars of arriving passengers, so a continuous twenty-four-hour repair operation was carried out, with both departing and arriving road traffic squeezed at first into the one remaining carriageway. The resulting delays were so severe that the cargo tunnel, opened only days before by Trade Minister William Rogers, was hurriedly pressed into service for passengers. The cracking tunnel lining was made good in nine days, just in time for the Christmas rush, but a basic weakness remained.

Radical strengthening and relining of both passenger tunnels was carried out over the next four and a half years, with the Customs again allowing public use of the cargo tunnel, to avoid airport road traffic grinding to a halt.

The 1957 Millbourn Committee had recommended a terminal for BEA on the north-east face of the Central Area parallelogram. Work started in 1966, and two years later the building opened, in a limited way at first, for domestic, Channel Islands and Ireland flights. The official inauguration was in April 1969, when the Queen revealed that, since she lived at Windsor, she was 'perhaps more conscious than many people of the immense and ever increasing volume' of Heathrow's traffic. Her Majesty named the new building 'Terminal 1'.

A few days later the Queen and the Duke of Edinburgh gave a further seal of approval to the new terminal, when they left from there for a two-day state visit to Austria. This departure made them the first international passengers to pass through Terminal 1. Two days later, the building was opened to all international passengers, when BEA moved in their European services, and Aer Lingus their flights to Ireland.

The £11 million terminal was the largest in Europe, and boasted stands for twenty aeroplanes. A road for buses ran right through the building. The interior spaces were more light and airy than anything previously designed for Heathrow, the vast first-floor departures concourse being particularly elegant. The slender brown-painted steel columns were used with a sophistication borrowed from German master architect Mies van der Rohe.

While departures were handled at first floor level, arrivals were processed on the ground floor. This segregation of arrivals and departures on different levels avoided congestion and made possible larger passenger flows. The lessons of years of mass passenger handling were being learned, and reflected in concrete and glass. Even road traffic was split up, with two-level road access to the front of the building.

Terminal 1 had no proper façade on the land side, as it was joined on here to its multi-storey car park. Instead, just the top of the building peeped out above steps of vehicle ramps, parked cars and – the lowest step – landscaped vegetation on the ground.

In her Terminal 1 inauguration speech, the Queen gave new names to the other two terminals. The Europa became Terminal 2, the Oceanic Terminal 3. In airport circles these labels are often shortened to T1, T2 and T3.

Throughout the 1960s, news had been coming from America of a revolutionary aeroplane being developed by Boeing at their west coast headquarters. Big enough to carry several hundred people at one time, the Boeing 747 was about to change the world's airports.

# 5
# 747

It began as a study for a logistics transport for the US Air Force, but by March 1966 it was clear to Boeing that they had themselves the blueprint for a civilian airliner which would leave the opposition gawping.

The Boeing board gave the project the green light, and work started on a new factory to build the monster. On 14 April, Pan Am made the launching order, for twenty-five aircraft. In July, Lufthansa and Japan Air Lines ordered three each, and by now the success of the plane was gathering momentum. In August BOAC ordered six.

On 30 September 1968 the first 747 was ceremonially rolled out of the assembly hanger. Present were twenty-six stewardesses, representing the airlines who had by now placed orders. In February, this machine lifted off from Boeing's Seattle runway for the first time, with the order book now swollen to 160. The first delivery, to Pan Am, took place on 12 December 1969.

The 747 was basically an enlarged version of the 707, with four engines similarly slung below the wings. But the 747 was the first and biggest of the 'wide-bodied' airliners. The earliest version could carry about 350 passengers, in seats ten abreast. The cabin was long enough to contain the entire 1903 flight by the pioneering Wright brothers! Echoing their earlier Stratocruiser, Boeing gave the 747 two decks, the small upper level being reached by a spiral staircase. With fuel for a long flight, the 747 would heave itself off the ground weighing as much as 370 tons. This momentous mass gave it stability in flight which passengers enjoyed as smoothness and absence of turbulence. The pilots, strapped into their tiny cockpit, rarely glimpsed the wings far behind them and, unable to judge the attitude of their aircraft by traditional sight, they had to rely more than ever on their instruments.

On taking up his BAA post, Peter Masefield had immediately flown to Boeing in Seattle to find out exactly what was going to be needed for the new plane. With some versions expected to carry 500 passengers, compared with about 170 for the 707, Masefield's mission was carried out with urgency. Designs were drawn up, and work was able to start on the new facilities after Runway 6 (15/33) was closed on 1 July 1968. So much space was going to be needed to park the 747, or 'Jumbo' as it was quickly nicknamed, that this runway had to be sacrificed, as foreseen by the Millbourn Committee. Its parallel partner, Runway 4, had already been withdrawn to provide more space in front of Terminal 1.

Work started on seven Jumbo stands on the closed runway. Each stand was to be equipped with what was variously termed a 'gate room', 'holding lounge', or even 'forward assembly area'. Here the hundreds of passengers who would wait to board each 747 would be able to sit down in an area of 4,500 square feet, while final preparations for boarding were made by the airline. The gate rooms were a new innovation for the Jumbo. Building them, was rather like equipping each 747 stand with its own departure lounge. They were linked to each other by a new pier – Pier 7 – which formed the cross-head of a T. The upright of the T was formed by another pier which linked Pier 7 to the terminal building itself. This upright of the T was 900 feet long and was fitted with two stretches of travelators, or moving walkways. This was the first time these devices had been seen at a

British airport, and at the time it was not technically possible to cover the whole 900 feet in one stretch.

To deal with peak flows when several Jumbos would arrive at the same time, the terminal building itself had to be enlarged. A separate structure solely for arriving passengers was introduced on the north side of Terminal 3, while the original 1962 building was converted to handle only departures, being relabelled 'Terminal 3 Departures'.

Meanwhile, the two runways 1 and 5 (09/27 Left and Right) had been extended. Carrying fuel for a long flight, the 747 was going

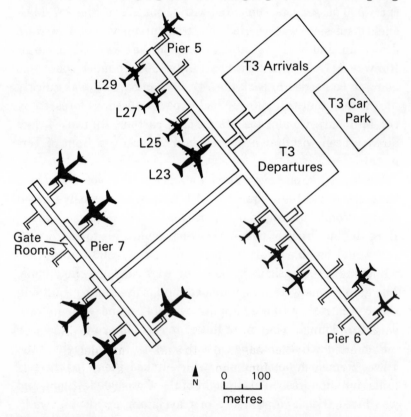

Terminal 3, 1970

to need that much more distance to haul itself off the concrete, and by April 1970 both strips were lengthened from 9,000 feet to around 12,000 feet. That's two and a quarter miles, a figure which has since been equalled by most of the world's major airports. The extension work was carried out while the runways remained in service, with screaming jets passing over the heads of workmen. The runway extensions were only 150 feet wide. Although the original lengths of runway were mostly a grand 300 feet in width, 150 feet had by now become accepted as the world standard, with any greater width deemed unnecessary, even disorientating and dangerous.

The first 747 arrived, from Kennedy Airport, New York, on 12 January 1970. Pan Am's Clipper 'Constitution' touched down in a blaze of publicity with 381 on board, made up of 19 crew and 362 passengers, most of them Pan Am employees on a free trip. This was a proving flight but nevertheless Peter Masefield was there, talking to the press, predicting that even bigger planes in the future would make the 747 look like the 707. 'Constitution' arrived late, and Masefield peered impatiently through the drizzle and mist as the giant docked.

It surprised many observers that passenger disembarkation went smoothly. The special giant stands for the 747 were not completed in time, and 'Constitution' was directed instead on to Stand L25. This was built for normal-sized aircraft, with a door sill height of about ten feet. The doors on the 747 are sixteen feet above the ground. To reach this extra height, temporary extensions had been fitted to the loading bridges. This improvised arrangement worked well, and the full Jumbo load of passengers was processed and reunited with their baggage with a minimum of delay.

The first scheduled Jumbo to bring in fare-paying passengers arrived nine days later, which was a whole day later than planned. Clipper 'Young America', christened by the wife of US President Richard Nixon, encountered its first problem when they couldn't get one of the cabin doors closed at Kennedy. Then strong winds during taxiing caused Number 4 Engine to stall and overheat, necessitating a return to the gate, and disembarkation of passengers during repairs. Not an auspicious start!

BOAC was among the first to get delivery of the 747, but the airline was unable to use its new aircraft because of industrial action. First the pilots, then the flight engineers refused to fly the Jumbo until they got more money. A compromise was negotiated in April 1971, and suddenly BOAC caught up with the wide-bodied era. There was one further delay, however, when departure of the first Jumbo was held up for three hours by a technical hitch over closing one of the doors.

The annual traffic figures for Heathrow were continuing to increase, and by the end of the '60s the vast majority of aircraft were jets, placing a terrible noise burden on local residents. Grants for double glazing and roof insulation were being made available, but their effectiveness obviously depended on people staying indoors and keeping their windows closed. Night flights were not normally permitted, but some complained that they still had to sleep with the bedroom windows closed because of early morning flights. During the day, conversations in the street were regularly interrupted by the dreaded roar. Protest groups became more numerous and militant, culminating in a particularly angry association known as CHAOS.

The initials stood for Close Heathrow Airport On Sundays. This imperative was to be given added weight by a blockade of the airport one Sunday in early 1970. The group's organizer, fifty-six-year-old Hampton publisher Gordon Landsborough, hoped his supporters would turn up on foot, on bicycles, and in cars, and then form an inpenetrable traffic jam centred on the roundabout at the entrance to the passenger tunnel.

On the chosen Sunday more than a hundred police were waiting. Landsborough had big hopes for his blockade, but as the

allotted time of 12 noon passed, a mere handful of cars ineffec-
tually circled the roundabout and were warned off by the police.
The bobbies had no need for the towing truck which they had
standing by. A disbelieving Mr Landsborough said he was bitterly disappointed, as thousands of people had written to him,
giving their support.

With a Conservative victory at the General Election, Edward
Heath became Prime Minister. The similarity of the new leader's
name to that of the country's principal airport gave rise to a
confusion in the minds of foreigners who based their assumptions
on La Guardia, Dulles and Kennedy. To this day, Mr Heath
remains without an airport named in his honour.

Heathrow and the other airports making up the BAA group
were joined by a fifth when Edinburgh Airport was handed over
to the Authority. It was in a sorry state, being little more than a
handful of shacks facing a badly aligned runway. The BAA were
expected to bring their new charge up to the standards they had
established elsewhere, and plans for a complete new runway,
aligned to prevailing winds, were already prepared. It was to be
built to the west, clear of the existing airfield, and a new terminal
area was to follow. Effectively the BAA were to build a whole new
airport at Edinburgh, an expensive scheme which was to milk
some of the profit from Heathrow for at least the next decade.

At the end of 1971 Peter Masefield resigned from the BAA. He
had guided the Authority through its birth and, after nearly six
years as chairman, left it profitable. During his reign rarely a
week passed without his finding a reason to visit the premier
airport in the group. An important achievement at Heathrow was
the improvement at last of relations between airport management and the airlines. Some critics, ignorant of both the RAF
origins of Heathrow and the constant need to adapt it to bigger
and more numerous aircraft, complained that the airport looked
like a perpetual building site. In reply, Masefield was never

apologetic. He liked to quote in reverse the normal sign on hoardings around building work: 'Alterations as usual during business'.

Masefield was replaced by Nigel Foulkes, the fifty-two-year-old managing director of Rank Xerox. While Masefield loved aeroplanes and Heathrow equally, his successor had no particular affection for either. Foulkes cheerfully admitted that all he knew about airports was the little he'd picked up by passing through them as a passenger. Although, during the war, he commanded a squadron of the RAF Regiment – similar to the Marines in the navy – he hadn't flown, and knew little about aircraft. Foulkes was offered the chairmanship not for his technical knowledge, but for his record as a manager. While Masefield ran the Authority with passion and commitment to aviation, Foulkes remained detached. Financial control and service to the customer were to be his two guiding principles. Foulkes management philosophy was founded on his conviction that the great weakness of British industry was to underestimate the importance of the market. He insisted that it was the customer who should shape the business, and he embarked on a crusade to change what he saw as bureaucratic attitudes blunting the responsiveness of the Authority. Foulkes considered that ex-civil servants, faced with the public, tended to dig themselves in. He felt that training had taught them to see the public not as customers, but as opponents making constant impossible demands upon the bureaucracy. Nigel Foulkes might know little of the workings of the silver bird, but he knew how to run a business, and he relished the chance to eradicate these entrenched attitudes.

In 1972 a terrible tragedy occurred very close to Heathrow. A BEA Trident took off in a westerly direction one Sunday afternoon in June. After a routine left turn, the leading edge slats on the wings were apparently retracted early, resulting in a stall. The plane fell out of the sky and struck the ground close to

Staines bypass. This is a largely built-up area, but fortunately nobody on the ground was hurt. All 118 aboard were killed. News broadcasts of the tragedy attracted thousands of curious onlookers who unwittingly hampered the emergency services.

Transport Minister Michael Heseltine announced on 2 July that a joint board would be established to supervise the activities of the two big British carriers, BEA and BOAC. Within a year this British Airways board announced that the two nationalized concerns were to merge completely. Gradually the aircraft of BEA and BOAC were repainted in the same red, white and blue, bearing the words 'British Airways'. With BA occupying most of Terminal 1 and a good slice of Terminal 3, the aesthetic impact of the new livery was most impressive at Heathrow, although there was public criticism a few years later, when the entire fleet was repainted in the same colours all over again, this time without the word 'Airways'. In bold serif lettering, BA aircraft now carried the single word 'British'. It seemed a daft idea at first, but there was no denying the impact of a big gleaming 747 on some foreign apron, proudly boasting that one majestic word. At the start of the '80s BA again changed their image, reinstating the 'Airways' and switching to modest capital letters on a pale grey fuselage.

To compete with Boeing's 747, the rival American manufacturers Lockheed and McDonnell-Douglas produced their own, less ambitious long-range wide-bodied jets. Their Tristar and DC-10 each had only three engines and could carry little more than half the passengers of the 747, but they found a market nevertheless. In 1971/72 there were 13,000 movements by wide-bodied jets at Heathrow. 1974 saw nearly twice that number, and a decade later the figure had almost trebled again. Their voluminous holds swallowed the passengers' luggage with ease, and still had room for an unprecedented amount of freight. The effects of this carrying capacity are all around us, but nowhere more so than on

British supermarket shelves. Exotic tropical vegetables and fruits are now readily available, cheap and fresh, having been flown here in a matter of hours.

Wide-bodied jets had an unforeseen effect on the Cargo Terminal. There has always been a school of aviation thought which believes that the future is brighter for pure freight airlines operating pure freight aircraft than it is for conventional passenger airlines. This view is a mirage which always shimmers on the horizon, but never materializes. Passenger planes today are able to carry so much that there is little need for freight-only aircraft. Of the twenty-six stands in the cargo area, usually only a handful are occupied. However, business does continue within the vast freight sheds here. Crates, containers and loose goods for export are delivered by road, sorted by the airline, and on the airside loaded not so much into aircraft as on to other lorries for carriage through the cargo tunnel. Once in the Central Area, they are driven straight to the freight doors of passenger planes. The loading operation is highly mechanized and does not delay departures.

The parallel runways 1 and 5 (09/27) were showing signs of wear, and the decision was taken to cover their original concrete surfaces with a top layer of asphalt in a process known as 'overslabbing'. The work was carried out at night, over several months, using quick-hardening asphalt. Early each morning the runways had to be back in service for the unrelenting schedule of aircraft movements. The width of the overslabbing was only 150 feet, so half the original width of these mighty runways is now redundant verge.

Britain was shocken by two incidents on the same day in 1974. Firstly a Turkish Airlines wide-bodied jet with 345 aboard crashed after taking off from Paris. It had not been noticed that a baggage hold door was not properly closed, and this caused the hold to lose pressurization, leading to the collapse of the cabin floor, and the severing of control lines. There were no survivors. More than half those aboard had been booked with British Airways, but industrial action by baggage handlers at Heathrow had led them to travel on the doomed DC–10 instead.

Also on 4 May, a much smaller British Airways airliner was hijacked and blown up by Palestinian terrorists. The VC–10 was returning to Heathrow from Bombay. After a stop at Beirut the mainly Pakistani and Indian passengers were settling down for the last leg of their journey when an Arab passenger rose to his feet with an automatic pistol, and pointed it down the aisle. Meanwhile an accomplice had forced his way into the cockpit and, with a pistol held to the co-pilot's back, ordered the captain and flight engineer to the rear of the plane. The terrorist in the cabin unloaded a large quantity of high explosives, and then spent a long time attaching fuses to a travel bag. Further explosives were unpacked from a shoe box, distributed around the aircraft, and fused. Over the North Sea the plane turned around and landed at Amsterdam Schiphol. The passengers had been remarkably calm until now, but they grew increasingly agitated as one of the terrorists took bottles of whisky from the duty-free store, smashed them on the floor, and emptied their inflammable contents over seats which had been wired up with explosives. The air inside the cabin filled with spirit fumes as the airliner stood alone in a remote corner of the Dutch airfield. Suddenly the passengers were told to get out by sliding down the chute which hung from one of the emergency exits. The two terrorists were not far behind them, and they almost escaped amidst the confusion. Minutes later the VC–10 was wrecked by a mighty explosion.

A fortnight later there was more terror when a man with an Irish accent phoned the Press Association in London, quoting an IRA code word.

'Now listen carefully. There is a bomb due to go off between 11.10 and 11.15 in the Heathrow car park.'

He hung up without saying which car park. The news agency immediately informed Scotland Yard, and police started to evacuate all likely targets. Industrial action by baggage handlers was causing some congestion that morning, and there was delay in getting everyone out of the four multi-storey car parks. Suddenly the bomb went off. It was in Terminal 1 car park, a 10lb device hidden in a Morris 1100 on the second floor. Fifty cars were wrecked or badly damaged by the explosion. Flying glass injured an American passenger, who needed stitches in his head. Fortunately he was the only casualty in this first terrorist outrage at the airport.

To police its airports, the BAA had, since its inception, maintained its own constabulary, with its own chief constable. The Chairman of the BAA was also the Chairman of the police authority. This system worked reasonably well until political terrorism began to pose a major threat to airlines and airports world-wide. In 1972 the BAA doubled its police and security staff. Metropolitan Police reinforcements were drafted into Heathrow. The tension steadily rose and, in January 1974, armed soldiers arrived in armoured personnel carriers, for several days of military exercises in and around the airport. In the year to April 1974, almost 300 people died in European and Middle East airports because of terrorists. Nigel Foulkes concluded that he needed organization and resources beyond the means of the BAA. It was impossible to combat international terrorists with small airport police forces confined by their perimeter fences. Foulkes asked Home Secretary Roy Jenkins for anti-terrorist work to be permanently assigned to police from outside the airports. The Home Office saw difficulties in separating the anti-terrorist function, and on 29 April 1974 Roy, Jenkins told the House of Commons:

'I do not consider that these duties can satisfactorily be divided from normal police work. As a result I have agreed that the

Metropolitan Police should assume responsibility for all policing at Heathrow.'

The hand-over took place six months later, followed a few months after that by a similar hand-over at the other airports in the BAA group. For Nigel Foulkes, businessman, being in charge of a police force had been a novel experience, and he privately admitted to relinquishing his police role with a sense of relief. His only slight concern was that the change might somehow upset the strained industrial relations that continued between baggage handlers, the various airlines who employed them, and the forces of law and order.

Back in 1971, just before Foulkes took over at the BAA, the Tory Government revealed their intention to prohibit further growth at both Heathrow and Gatwick, and to close Stansted altogether. Instead new growth would be encouraged at a new super-airport to be built on the Maplin Sands in Essex, at a spot known as Foulness. Planned to open in 1980, Maplin Airport would have an ultimate capacity of 125 million passengers a year. It was an incredibly exciting prospect, and it rather put Heathrow in the shade. Maplin was to be served by new motorways, and by a new high-speed surface rail link with central London. There would be four runways, all of them aligned in the same north-east to south-west direction. With the airport at the end of a peninsula, all aeroplane approach and departure routes would be over water, making it environmentally acceptable for Maplin to operate around the clock.

Nigel Foulkes described the project as 'the first environmental airport'. Sited on land expensively reclaimed from sea and marsh, it would be well away from any noise-sensitive populated areas. Such was the strength of environmentalist sentiment in the early 1970s, that even this barren site was considered too precious, even though most of it lay beneath the North Sea. Ecologists gravely pronounced that the scheme would make some marsh birds homeless.

With the dramatic rise in the price of oil which started in 1973, and the world recession which followed, concern with the environment waned. In the end it was harsh economic reality, rather than the fate of marsh birds, which defeated Maplin Airport. Labour came to power in 1974, and the new Government cancelled the whole project.

During the Foulkes years there occurred an astonishing reversal when, in 1974/75, for the first time in the history of Heathrow, the number of passengers using the airport actually fell. The quadrupled price of oil had increased the cost of flying, while the down-turn in economic activity reduced demand for travel. Revenue from landing fees was threatened, as airlines sought to fly a few full aeroplanes rather than lots of half-empty ones.

1975 opened with the hijack of another British Airways plane, this time within British airspace. The little 1–11 was seized by a single Iranian gunman, on a flight from Manchester. At Heathrow he told the forty-five passengers to please move to the front and disembark, before he began bargaining with police in the control tower. He demanded £100,000, enough fuel to reach Paris, and a parachute. The plane was refuelled, a parachute was brought from Northolt, and eventually he was given the money. After being held at gunpoint at Heathrow for nearly eight hours, the crew were relieved to be able to take off shortly after 10 p.m. The hijacker thought he was going to Paris, but in fact the plane was headed for Stansted, where an emergency disguise was being put into operation. British vehicles were hidden, English language signs removed and lights turned off. Once the plane landed the police disarmed the man, only to find that his gun was a toy.

On the Heathrow–Glasgow route British Airways launched, for the first time in Europe, an American-style shuttle service with no booking, and a seat guaranteed for anyone turning up. If all the seats on the plane were taken, the airline would bring in a second machine, even if it was only needed for one passenger! The shuttle was introduced on 12 January, and on 1 February the concept was developed further, with tickets for the flight being sold by cabin staff actually on board the aeroplane. This time-saving improvement was immediately threatened by a clerical workers' strike, although negotiations did eventually allow the practice to continue.

In 1975 Glasgow and Aberdeen airports joined the BAA, bringing the number of airports in the group to seven, as it remains today. The Authority was now responsible for the three London airports (Heathrow, Gatwick and Stansted), and four in Scotland (Prestwick, Edinburgh, Glasgow and Aberdeen). Over the years the newcomers were to benefit from the big profits made at Heathrow. Aberdeen was notable for being both Britain's fastest-growing airport and the world's busiest heliport. Most of its traffic was generated by the North Sea oil and gas industries.

Terminal 2 was now twenty years old, and a programme of building improvements was started. The work caused a lot of annoyance, but it had to be done because circulation problems between the ground and first floors were badly restricting passenger through-put. The most visible alteration was on the landside façade, where two zigzag pedestrian ramps were hung on the outside of the building. Looking like plastic tubes, these ramps were covered in with brilliant white glass fibre. Walking through one of them was rather like pushing your baggage trolley around the giant intestine of some primeval plastic monster.

The 1.2 per cent drop in passenger numbers in 1974/75 was followed by an encouraging 6.3 per cent rise the following year, and then a healthy 9.6 per cent rise the year after that. Things were almost back to normal. Small decreases in passenger figures did occasionally recur in subsequent years, but the overall upward trend was re-established.

The financial year 1976/77 saw Heathrow overtake the Port of London, to become the busiest port in Britain in terms of value of goods carried.

# 6
# Concorde

At the same moment on 21 January 1976, both Heathrow and Charles de Gaulle airport near Paris saw the world's first departures of supersonic aircraft. While British Airways Concorde registration letters G-BOAA was lined up for its take-off run at Heathrow, a similar machine belonging to Air France stood at the end of the runway at de Gaulle. On board the BA Concorde, the hundred expectant passengers included the Duke of Kent and Trade Minister Peter Shore, together with journalists, senior engineers and thirty-five fare-paying members of the public. For five minutes they waited in position at the end of the runway for the pre-arranged take-off time. Dozens of subsonic carriers were put behind schedule, and among those behind Concorde in the queue for take-off were Pan-Am and TWA, both of whom had cancelled options to buy the plane.

In the cockpit Captain Norman Todd sat with his right hand poised on the thrust levers of the four Olympus engines. In the French machine Captain Pierre Dudal did likewise, with British test pilot Brian Trubshaw in the co-pilot seat. As 11.40 approached, both crews were given a count-down over the radio. Five. Four. Three, Two. One. Zero. Both captains pushed their thrust levers fully forward. In a gesture symbolic of equal partnership, the British and French machines roared into life, accelerated along the ground for thirty-five seconds, and took to the air at the same instant. The supersonic era was born. For their first flight, Air France raced towards Dakar and Rio de Janiero, while the BA Concorde pointed its sleek nose towards unlikely Bahrain. Passengers eagerly eyed the Machometer in the cabin as the plane accelerated them towards Mach 1, the speed of sound. The flight went according to plan, but the Machometer got stuck at 0.7, despite efforts to thump it into life.

Concorde flies faster than a bullet, at Mach 2.05, more than twice the speed of sound. Cruising height is on the edge of space, at 60,000 feet, where the sky is dark blue, and the curvature of the earth is discernible in the horizon. At this altitude there is scant atmosphere to protect the plane from space radiation, and indeed a cosmic ray meter is included on the instrument panel. At full speed considerable heat is generated in the skin of the aircraft, and passengers with a window seat have remarked that it's rather like having your head next to a radiator. Thermal expansion causes a Concorde at speed to increase its own length by nine inches. The delta wings make it necessary for the plane to land and take off at high speed, causing ATC complications, and the long nose has to be drooped at such times so that the pilots can see the ground. The Concorde was built jointly by Britain and France, with final assembly lines at both Bristol and Toulouse. The wings and the engines were contributed by Britain.

A prestigious Concorde check-in area was provided in Terminal 3, together with a luxurious Concorde lounge. As far away as the M4 spur, road signs highlighted the way for Concorde passengers. The plane itself was given a convenient stand right next to the Departures building. People flying out on Concorde were not expected to walk very far!

The deafening row made by Concorde's four Rolls-Royce engines caused concern in the surrounding communities. It had seemed that jet engines were getting quieter. Since the original pure jet engines of the Comet and the 707, the arrival of the quieter turbofan jets of the 747 and other wide-bodied aircraft had continued to reduce steadily the overhead roar to something more like a hum. The fan in these engines throws out a layer of unheated, slower air around the central core of fast and hot gases that blast out of the back of the turbine. This slower air acts like a cushion, preventing the raw exhaust gases from rubbing up against stationary air, thereby generating that awful roar. The trouble with Concorde was that it didn't have turbofans.

As it turned out, the residents needn't have worried. Only fourteen Concordes were ever sold, compared to 600 sales of the 747, and no influx of any other kind of supersonic pure jets has materialized either. The high price of oil worked against fuel-hungry supersonic flying, and only the routes to Washington and New York made money – after the Government had written off the capital cost to British Airways.

In 1979 the regular service to Bahrain was extended to Singapore, with an eye to an eventual money-spinning extension to Australia, but Bahrain and Singapore themselves got the chop in 1980. 1979 saw Braniff Airlines introduce an extension to the Washington route, with Braniff crews flying Concorde on to Dallas, but this too was dropped in 1980.

Charters have turned out to be a consolation prize for Concorde, with endless novelty flights and day trips to exotic places bringing in a modest income. For example, every year the organizers of the British motor racing Grand Prix include a fly-past by Concorde in the day's programme. American golfers competing in The Open annually roar over the course on their way in from the States. Shipping lines use Concorde as a suitably luxurious vehicle for taking cruise passengers to and from their liners in the Caribbean. Even Halley's Comet and the eclipse of the sun have been used to drum up business.

Despite its disappointing sales record, Concorde retains its glamour. Indeed, commercial failure has had the effect of preserving the rarity value of the plane, while increasing the prestige of

Heathrow, which handles more Concorde movements than any other airport. The high number of sleek supersonics among the lumbering subsonics is one reason that Heathrow today is the most exciting airport in the world.

The annual number of people passing through Heathrow reached 24,000,000 in 1976/77. Those passengers who arrived by road were finding it increasingly difficult to fight their way through the passenger tunnel. At peak periods there were usually queues of traffic waiting to get into the airport, and the Central Area often resembled one huge traffic jam. Work on a desperately needed Heathrow Underground link was at last under way, and in the meantime traffic flows into the airport were helped by opening the inbound pedestrian tunnel to taxis. Those taxi drivers who wish to pick up a fare at the airport have to report to the 'feeder park' on the airport perimeter, where they have to wait until summoned to the Central Area. This system prevents the terminal forecourts from becoming congested. With the new taxi route through the tunnel it was now less likely that a passenger could fly into Heathrow and be unable to find a cab.

Chairman Nigel Foulkes found his job at the BAA more interesting than he had expected. While he continued to frown upon those considered to have a civil service attitude towards the public, at the same time he was entertained by the enthusiasm of his colleagues for aviation itself. Foulkes knew well that there were many industries where people hate their work and would be glad to get out of it. But in aviation everybody seemed to love their industry. The danger was that enthusiasm could go too far, becoming romantic optimism, and producing commercial disaster amongst those believing that they would somehow make money just by putting the silver bird into the sky.

Foulkes left the BAA on 1 March 1977, after running the Authority for five years. He had proved a sound financial helmsman during the economic storms of the '70s. He now moved to the

chairmanship of the less commercial, more regulatory, Civil
Aviation Authority.

Effectively Foulkes picked his own successor and groomed him
for the post. Fifty-five-year-old Norman Payne had risen on the
engineering side of the BAA. In 1965 he had been appointed
Director of Engineering, and in 1969 Director of Planning,
becoming a member of the Board two years after that.

During Payne's term as Chairman, the strength of the environmental lobby was to decline further. When a nation is rich it can
afford environmentalism. In leaner times the environmental
pressures tend to be seen as secondary and possibly fanciful. Then
the stark business of making a profit and keeping the wolf from
the door takes precedence. As British dole queues lengthened, it
became less fashionable to see airports as a threat, more as
important cogs in the economy and providers of employment.

Freddie Laker started his cut-price 'Skytrain' service from Gatwick to New York on 26 September 1977. The no-frills, no-
booking service attracted world-wide publicity, with Skytrain
perceived as the beginning of the end for price-fixing and airline
cartels. Cockney Freddie Laker was the champion of free enter-
prise, a Robin Hood figure pitted against the rich airlines, the
man to share with his customers the generous benefits of wide-
body economics. The BAA had long been attempting to persuade
reluctant airlines to leave the congestion of Heathrow for the
West Sussex spaciousness of Gatwick. Now the Laker razzmatazz
at last gave Gatwick some much-needed glamour. The first-ever
Skytrain ticket was sold at 4 a.m. in front of ten television camera
crews and fifty reporters. The media arrived in even greater
numbers for the departure of the plane itself, a DC–10 with a
livery of pop graphics combining the Union Jack and the Stars
and Stripes.

By now only airlines already established there were allowed to
use Heathrow. There was no room left for newcomers because the

runways, the aprons and particularly the terminals were operating at full capacity for longer and longer periods of the day. Airlines introducing London into their schedules for the first time were forced to use Gatwick, the home of many charter carriers and the rapidly growing British Caledonian, as well as Laker. Over the years Delta, American, Air New Zealand and Cathay Pacific would all fall into this category. One particularly interesting newcomer which Heathrow lost to Gatwick because of this situation was People Express, the highly democratic US concern in which the lowliest cleaner took a turn at being a manager. And once again Gatwick was undeniably the centre of attention when British pop tycoon Richard Branson launched his 'Virgin Atlantic' line, with a fleet of one leased 747! By comparison the establishment carriers at Heathrow looked staid.

Besides proximity to London and the glamour of the place, the great appeal of Heathrow for the airlines lay in the fact that it was already extremely busy. This increased the scope for 'interlining', that is to say the business of passengers proceeding from A to B with one airline, and then changing to a second airline for the journey to their final destination, C. Interlining can increase passenger loads on a given route by crucial points.

At Gatwick, which was only handling about one tenth of the number of scheduled passengers passing through Heathrow, there was less opportunity to pick up extra business in this way. There wasn't much the BAA could do about this, except try to improve the status of Gatwick, by describing its role as one of equal partnership with Heathrow. The authority back-pedalled on the name 'London Airport' for example, stressing again and again that Heathrow, Gatwick and Stansted were all 'the London airports', making up 'the London airport system'. Just as the full name of Gatwick was 'Gatwick Airport, London', so Heathrow was no longer 'London Airport', but rather 'Heathrow Airport, London'.

Public transport to Heathrow was transformed with the opening in December 1977 of an extension of the London Underground network right into the heart of the airport. Key London locations such as Knightsbridge, Mayfair, Covent Garden and King's Cross Station were brought within an hour of the terminals.

The Piccadilly Line, which had ended three miles from Heathrow, at Hounslow West, was now extended in a cut-and-cover tunnel beneath the A30, coming to the surface briefly to cross the little River Crane. A new station was built at Hatton Cross to serve the maintenance area, and this was opened first, in 1975. West of Hatton Cross the new line swung away from the A30, descended into a deep tube, and burrowed beneath the airfield. In the Central Area the tunnel emerged into a new subterranean station a few yards north of the control tower. From here pedestrian subways equipped with travelators radiate to the three terminals.

With road congestion what it is, the Underground is the quickest way of getting to Heathrow from central London at most times of day. Heavy suitcases are a problem, but it's an interesting ride for much of the journey, with the eight miles from Hammersmith to Hounslow passing through surprisingly leafy suburbs.

This was the first time that a major world airport was connected to an urban underground rail system. The quickest way from Manhattan to Kennedy Airport remains by taxi along the congested and optimistically named Long Island Expressway. From Paris, once you've fought your way to Gare du Nord, there is a fast train to de Gaulle but, incredibly, the airport station is sited so that passengers have to pile on to a bus to reach the actual terminals.

So Heathrow took the lead in surface links, although there was one disappointment. It had been hoped that the Piccadilly Line would make life easier for those passengers continuing to travel to and from the airport by road. In fact the opening of the tube had surprisingly little impact on the congestion in the road tunnel. After a lull of only months, the morning and evening traffic peaks were back at their old levels, with taxis belching diesel fumes still being allowed to take over the inbound pedestrian tunnel.

Despite the Underground, 20 per cent of passengers still use taxis to get to and from Heathrow, where the provision and administration of the feeder park costs the BAA £600,000 per annum. In 1985 they imposed a 50-pence charge on each cab to recoup their expenses, and the drivers responded by boycotting Heathrow, arguing that they could not afford the new charge. The BAA countered that the money had to come from somewhere, and if it came out of landing charges then all passengers would effectively be subsidising the minority who travel by taxi. The cabbies challenged the 50p charge in the High Court, but in due course the charge was held to be legal.

The BAA saw the opening of the Heathrow-Gatwick Airlink in 1978 as another sweetener for airlines banished to West Sussex. Now the strength of the arguments about needing to be based at Heathrow for its inter-airline connections were weakened. This British Caledonian helicopter service provided ten flights in each direction every day, carrying 60,000 passengers in its first year. The chopper was popular with businessmen because it was quick and also rather exciting, however pricey. There were noise objections from residents under the helicopter flight path, and these became more vociferous years later when the M25 was completed, connecting the two airports by motorway. The objectors argued that motorway coaches should do the job and that the helicopters should be stopped, while the BAA retorted that their important passengers were accustomed to helicopters and would not take kindly to a mere bus. The Government decided in favour of the objectors, and in February 1986 the Heathrow–Gatwick Airlink was withdrawn.

The number of passengers passing through Heathrow was still rising, despite a ban on charter flights effective from April 1978. Pressure was particularly acute in Terminal 3, where just seven jumbos could account for the terminal's entire capacity for an hour. The surge in the long-haul figures was produced by two key sectors, Middle East and transatlantic. Middle East flows expanded an astounding 40 per cent in 1977/78 alone, as the energy crisis boosted oil-related business traffic, and as new oil wealth encouraged Arab leisure travel. The transatlantic sector expanded because of Laker's introduction of low stand-by fares, a ploy hurriedly emulated by the several other carriers operating the water jump.

Stand-by tickets brought fresh problems for Heathrow. In the summer of 1978 crowds of sedentary stand-by seekers caused quite a jam in Terminal 3. Most of them were carefree youngsters, with apparently little money but bags of time, so much time that many of them waited in the terminal for days. Seats were taken over and large areas of floor monopolized. The nation's intercontinental gateway was beginning to look like a squatters' encampment. Though well meaning, stand-by passengers inevitably inconvenienced more conformist travellers, who expected to move through the terminal at speed, without tripping over some denim-clad back-packer asleep on the floor. The airlines were asked to restrict stand-by sales to outside the Central Area. When TWA and Air India persisted, the BAA obtained a High Court injunction to stop them.

It's bad enough to be involved at all in what the rescue people call an 'incident', but for anyone doubly unfortunate and finding themselves crashing into the sewage works, the BA now made special provision, with the purchase of the 'Tortoise'. This amphibious rescue machine can climb in and out of the Perry Oaks sewage lagoons, and its huge wheels allow it to thrash about messily but effectively on the surface.

A tiny bit of extra capacity was wrung from the Central Area with the opening in 1981 of the Eurolounge, a communal gate room for the short high-density routes to Brussels, Amsterdam and especially Paris, London–Paris being the world's busiest international route. The Eurolounge and its five stands were squeezed in between Terminals 1 and 2, on the apron in front of the Queen's Building, and the complex was linked by travelator to both terminals. The travelator ride is a rather depressing experience, along joyless prefabricated corridors as appropriate for cattle as fare-paying passengers. Making long piers appear warm and friendly it not easy or cheap. Elsewhere at Heathrow such spaces managed to avoid the worst pitfalls, but with the Eurolounge the long corridor seemed to have descended to new depths of sensual deprivation.

Britain's conflict with Argentina over the sovereignty of the Falkland Islands reduced traffic between Heathrow and South America. The 1982 war generated resentment towards Britain throughout most of the continent, and there was a consequent fall in business and holiday traffic, compounded by weakness in some Latin economies.

This wasn't altogether bad news as it at least eased the mounting pressure on Terminal 3, pressure which had already driven British Airways to transfer their Miami and Chicago flights to Terminal 1. Over the years El Al and South African Airways were to follow, preferring the relative calm and safety of the short-haul terminal to the frequent overcrowding in long-haul.

With so many valuables passing through the airport, both as freight and passenger luggage, it's not surprising that there was crime at Heathrow. When baggage handlers repeatedly stole from bags and suitcases, the popular press dubbed the airport 'Thief-row'. Efforts to identify culprits were continually thwarted by animosity towards the police. When they proposed to search workers in suspicious circumstances, officers were often threatened with a protest strike which would bring the airport grinding to a halt.

In October 1985 West German showjumper Alwin Schocke-moehle was leaving Britain after successfully competing here. In his executive case he was carrying two watches, a shirt and £3,400 in cash. He was concerned about carrying such valuables, so checked in his case as baggage for the hold. When he arrived in Germany and was reunited with his case he found that the combination locks had been ripped off. All he found inside was the shirt. When the Metropolitan Police subsequently failed to make any headway with their investigations they cited 'union problems'.

There was also crime around the perimeter, where trading estates abound, lined with the warehouses of countless shippers, forwarders and agents dealing in air freight. The biggest robbery in British history was perpetrated on one such trading estate in Green Lane near Hatton Cross, when early on Saturday morning, 26 November 1983, a gang of six men drove away from the Brinks-Mat high security warehouse with three tons of gold. The 6,800 variously sized bars were valued at £26,000,000, which was twice the haul of the Great Train Robbers, even with inflation allowed for.

The gang entered the unmarked yellow brick and brown metal building despite an array of closed circuit TV cameras and electronic gadgetry. They handcuffed the six guards inside and singled out one of them for a particularly horrible threat. They slashed open the front of his uniform and poured petrol over his body. If he or his colleagues attempted to obstruct the raiders, the man was told, he would be set alight.

In 1984 Libyan dissidents were demonstrating peacefully outside their embassy in London when suddenly they came under a hail of machine-gun bullets. None of the demonstrators was killed but a policewoman was. Very strong evidence suggested that the shots had come from a first floor window of the embassy, and the building was surrounded by armed police. The occupants refused to allow the police to enter, and insisted on full diplomatic immunity. The situation developed into a police siege lasting several days, during which Britain's relations with Colonel Gadaffi's regime became tense. During the siege a time-bomb was left in a suitcase outside an unclaimed baggage area in Terminal 2, and when it exploded at 7.55 p.m. it injured 22 people, two of them seriously. It was the second time a terrorist bomb had exploded at Heathrow. Libyan involvement was suspected, and forensic evidence later revealed that the 2lb device was indeed similar to other Libyan bombs.

Middle East terrorists again shocked the world when they sprayed machine-gun bullets over crowds in the terminal buildings of Vienna and Rome airports. These two simultaneous attacks were aimed at passengers checking in with El Al. Within weeks the check-in areas at Heathrow were being patrolled by policemen with Heckler and Koch machine-guns. Airport police had sometimes carried concealed pistols, but this was the first time the British Bobby was seen toting a machine-gun. Scotland Yard argued that the weapons were essential to 'take out' a terrorist quickly. Home Secretary Douglas Hurd emphasized that the officers were under written instruction to use the weapons only in the 'single shot' mode. One expert nevertheless grabbed the headlines by pronouncing the Heckler and Koch unsuitable for use inside a crowded building. Its bullets, he warned, could ricochet, or pass right through their target.

# 7
# Terminal 4

The rapid expansion of the Central Area in the 1950s and '60s had been followed by a period of consolidation. For seventeen years no new terminal had been built, although the existing ones had resounded constantly to hammers and drills as they were modified, altered, enlarged, and probably modified again. With the spread of wide-bodied aircraft to all three terminals the concrete aprons had had to be strengthened. The increased wing span of the big jets had meant that the stands had had to be spaced out. This entailed repositioning gate rooms and installing new loading bridges. The end result was often fewer but larger stands on a pier, their fat fuselaged occupants disgorging ever greedier passenger loads.

The struggle to keep up with passenger demand now moved out of the Central Area. The three terminals there were by now handling 30,000,000 passengers a year. 125 aircraft stands had been squeezed in. It seemed there was hardly a square yard of concrete that didn't have a plane parked on it. Closing Runway Two would have allowed expansion eastwards, but this third runway was considered vital for crosswinds and emergencies. Instead the British Airports Authority pressed ahead with an idea they'd had on the back burner since the early '70s. Expansion now took place on the south-east perimeter of the airfield, close to the spot where Cain's Lane meets the Great South West Road. With zero imagination but admirable logic the new terminal was named Terminal 4. It incorporated two design concepts new to Heathrow.

Firstly, there is complete segregation of arriving and departing passengers. Departures on the top floor, arrivals on the floor below. Terminal 1 had used this idea to a limited extent, but there the two opposing flows still clash in the piers, testing tempers sometimes, and eliciting the odd annoying exchange. In streamlined Terminal 4, baggage trolleys can be taken right through the system. All routes are either level or gently downhill, and the two-level segregation of passengers continues all the way to the start of the loading bridge that leads to the aircraft door. As well as oiling the flow of passengers, segregation also makes flying from Heathrow a little safer. Terrorists cannot smuggle weapons from one flight to another, as has sometimes happened before hijackings over the eastern Mediterrranean.

The second Terminal 4 design innovation is the exclusion of piers. Instead the departure lounge has itself been stretched into one enormous room a third of a mile long. Ramps running down to the loading bridges lead directly off this lounge, and there are no separate gate rooms. The concept has much in common with small rural airports where passengers for various flights are summoned from a single lounge. What is so startling about the Terminal 4 design is the application of this system to a terminal handling up to 4,000 arriving and departing passengers an hour. An essential part of the system is the long line of travelators inside the lounge, which speed these thousands of people to the right part of the room for them to find the gate for their particular flight.

What the airport call 'weepers' are a common cause of congestion in check-in areas. In the worse cases Granny, Aunty Mabel, the kids and the family dog all come along to bid farewell to the one member of the family who is actually travelling. Invariably they leave it until the last minute before parting with their loved ones. Gently to curtail these obstructive farewell sessions the check-in concourse at Terminal 4 has deliberately been left stark and uncluttered. There are only a couple of small shops, very few seats, no carpets and little decoration. The exposed structural pipework overhead, the hard surfaces all around, the businesslike row of seventy-two airline desks, all these elements subtly discourage people from feeling at home or settling down to a long conversation here. Once through security and passport control, passengers find this bareness replaced by sumptuous luxury in the departure lounge.

The new terminal enjoys road links which are often faster than those leading to the Central Area, because there is no tunnel to act as a bottleneck. Terminal 4 backs on to the A30 Great South West Road, and a two-level interchange here provides quick access for central London traffic. In the other direction, the airport's sleepy southern perimeter road has been widened to four lanes, to form a speedy link from the terminal to the M25 London orbital motorway – Britain's busiest road. This section of the M25 is eight lanes wide and was finished just in time for the terminal's opening. It connects with motorways radiating from the capital to all parts of the country.

London Transport further extended the Piccadilly Line to give Terminal 4 its own tube station. A single track tunnel was bored from Hatton Cross to the Central Area via Terminal 4, to form a big loop at the end of the line. Around the loop, trains travel one-way in a clockwise direction. They arrive at Hatton from central London, as before, then take the new section of line to Terminal 4, continue round to the Central Area, return to Hatton, and finally set off back to central London. The Central Area station, formerly 'Heathrow Central', was renamed 'Heathrow Terminals 1, 2 and 3'.

With its own road and tube, Terminal 4 is like an airport within an airport, and the BAA were anxious to get this point across to the public. Before the opening 10,000 British and foreign travel trade representatives were shown around the

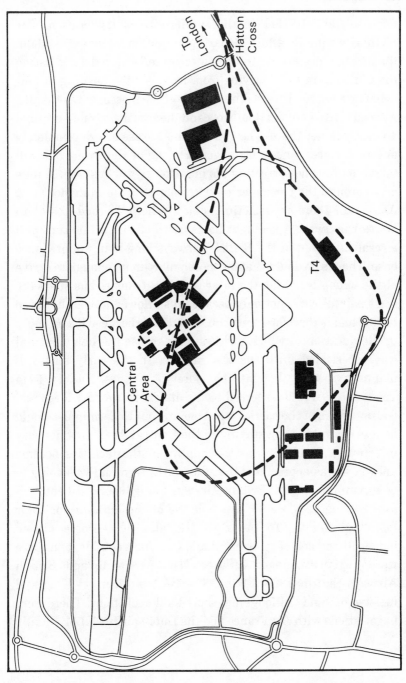

The Underground loop

terminal, and briefed on the significance of its location. The Authority's public affairs department bought whole-page ads in the national press, describing how to get to Terminal 4 and listing the flights soon to be leaving from it, under the heading 'A new departure for Heathrow'. The essence of the message was that it's no good setting out for Heathrow and then trying to find Terminal 4 when you get there. The two terminal areas are in completely different places, and a passenger arriving at the wrong one will take a lot of time correcting his mistake. By car it's a three mile drive around the perimeter road, through the maintenance area. Along here there are sometimes delays where the road crosses an aircraft taxiway. A red light holds up the traffic while tugs pull aircraft in or out of the British Airways long-haul maintenance base. There's no doubt that for those unfortunate enough to arrive at the wrong terminal, the inter-terminal transfer bus offers the least painful cure, not only because it's allowed to use the cargo tunnel and is therefore pretty quick, but also because it's free.

The question of which airlines were to use the new terminal was not settled until the last minute. In the early stages of planning it was thought that foreign airlines, mainly from Terminal 3, would be forced to use it. There was a widespread feeling amongst the carriers that moving out to Terminal 4 would be less desirable than staying in the Central Area, with its easy interlining. Gradually, as the quality of the facilities became known, it was appreciated that the fourth terminal was going to be something special. British Airways finally expressed enthusiasm, saying they would like sole use of the building for their long-haul flights. To the BAA the idea of a single airline monopolizing one of their terminals was unacceptable, and there were angry exchanges between Norman Payne and British Airways chairman Lord King. The BAA stood up to King and insisted on a mix of long- and short-haul operations. There were negotiations with Air France and the Dutch airline KLM. Finally the announcement came in June 1985 that Terminal 4 was to be shared by British Airways and KLM. British Airways would predominate, with all their long-haul flights, including Concorde, and their flights to Paris and Amsterdam. KLM brought with them their subsidiary, NLM City Hopper, and Air Malta, for whom they are the ground handler at Heathrow.

The emergence of this motley selection finally removed any trace of logic from the system. For more than a decade it had been simplicity itself to choose the right terminal at Heathrow.

T1: British and Irish airlines to Europe.
T2: European airlines to Europe.
T3: Outside Europe.

Cracks had first appeared in this simple arrangement with the transfers of Air Cyprus, SAA, El Al and flights to Chicago and Miami. With Terminal 4 the baffling allocation can best be summarized like this.

T1: British and Irish airlines to Europe, except British Airways to Paris
    and Amsterdam;
    Air Cyprus;
    El Al;
    SAA;
    Sabena.
T2: European airlines to Europe except Air Cyprus, Sabena, KLM and
    Air Malta.
T3: Outside Europe except British Airways, El Al and SAA.
T4: British Airways flights outside Europe, and to Paris and Amsterdam;
    KLM;
    NLM;
    Air Malta.

'Europe' in this context is generally understood to include the North African countries of Morocco, Algeria, Tunisia and Libya, which all lie within easy reach of short-haul aircraft.

In 1983 the BAA put up what they boasted in their annual report was the world's largest free-standing sign. This magnificent superlative was erected in front of the Terminal 4 building site so that it could be read by passengers on board aircraft or in the Central Area. Beside a giant BAA logo was proclaimed in letters six feet high: 'Terminal 4 opens 1985'. This illuminated record-breaking sign was quietly removed before the actual opening – in 1986.

The formal ceremonies were performed by the Prince and Princess of Wales on the morning of April Fool's Day. The future King and Queen arrived by tube, travelling from Hatton Cross with the driver in his cab. The journey gave the royal seal of approval to what some might have regarded as a plebeian mode of transport. In the subterranean booking hall, the Prince opened the new station with difficulty. His left arm was supported by a sling to protect his finger, following an accident hammering in a stake to support a tree at his home. Amidst laughter the Princess helped him fit the uninjured fingers of his other hand into a pair of scissors, so that the ceremonial ribbon could be severed.

The royal couple then set out on an exhaustive tour of the building, accompanied by Norman Payne and Lord King. The Princess wore a vaguely oriental, maroon and purple outfit with a white ruffle at the neck. Prince Charles' left arm was supported by a navy blue sling which matched his blazer, discreetly disguising his injury. With several days to go until the opening of the building to passengers, there were nevertheless large numbers of workers present, to give some impression of the terminal in operation. Check-in, shop and catering staff were all in position, and the cleaning contractors performed a curious 'March past' of vacuum cleaners. Charles and Di walked through a security metal detector arch, and enjoyed a ride on a travelator while their detectives walked alongside. They were presented with a couple of Harry Heathrow teddy bears to take home to their two sons, Prince Charles playfully finding a home for one of the bears in his sling. At the end of the thorough tour Princess Diana said it was nice to sit down. Charles suggested that the distances passengers have to march through terminals is designed to ensure that when they climb into the aircraft they are so exhausted that they fall asleep instantly and feel no more pain for the rest of the flight. His Royal Highness admitted that his own experience of airports was 'limited to the VIP lounge'.

The day chosen to bring the new terminal into operation was Saturday 12 April. Throughout the Friday all British Airways long-haul flights arrived and departed from Terminal 3 as usual, but from the start of flights on the 12th the move to Terminal 4 was complete. This remarkably swift feat was achieved by 'Operation Overnight', a meticulously planned transfer of air-craft, equipment, cars, buses, vans, lorries, and all the para-phernalia of a major airline base. Nearly 1,000 vehicles were used. Throughout the night, convoys made the journey across the airfield, with long lines of headlights stretching into the night. Men and machines negotiated taxiways, crossed Runway 5, and converged on their new home. At dawn all runways were able to open for the normal start time of flights. The first scheduled aeroplane to arrive at Terminal 4 was the 5.45 a.m. Jumbo from Bangladesh. The first passenger to emerge was a bleary-eyed businessman who found himself appearing on national television, with a British Airways official making a congratulatory speech. For being the first passenger to arrive at Terminal 4, the busi-nessman was presented with a free return ticket to the desti-nation of his choice.

The introduction of Terminal 4 fundamentally changed the shape of Heathrow Airport. For twenty-four years all passenger operations had been concentrated in the Central Area. This had been a tidy and satisfying state of affairs, in a sense spoiled now by the 'bit left over' on the south-east perimeter.

Because of Terminal 4's position there are new problems for ground controllers. Airliners using the terminal have to cross Runway 5 to get to or from Runway 1. For much of the day Runway 5 has an aeroplane landing every ninety seconds, and it can be difficult to get the traffic across. The situation is not without an element of danger. There is also a small financial penalty for Terminal 4 users, because they burn fuel while waiting for a gap in the landing pattern, before they get the go-ahead to nip across. The problem is not entirely new. In the old days, planes using the North Terminal had to cross Runway 1 to reach 5. But in those days traffic was light. Then the opening of the Cargo Terminal produced a similar situation in the south. But the number of freighters has never been large, and they tend to avoid busy periods when landing charges are higher. With the opening of Terminal 4, for the first time large numbers of airliners packed with people were having to taxi across a busy runway.

Despite its faults, most of them related to the site, Terminal 4 is a success and an asset to the airport. After the banality of the Eurolounge piers, the stylish £200,000,000 complex came as a treat. The international architectural firm of Scott, Brownrigg and Turner created the building from an original concept by BAA's own engineers. This was the first big passenger terminal not designed by Frederick Gibberd. SB&T were chosen from four big practices invited by the BAA to compete for the job. The design team toured the world's airports in search of ideas, and returned determined to introduce natural light into their building. Ann Gibson masterminded much of the detail, and she has produced a beautiful departure lounge which makes people gasp when they first see it. The outside of the building is given a silvery space-age skin, excitingly punctuated by yellow corrugated metal loading bridges and associated nodes and corridors. Inside, the building unashamedly has its guts on show, with structural members, heating ducts and water pipes all dangling above the heads of passengers. This hi-tech exposure owes much to Richard Rogers' Pompidou Centre in Paris. Architects call this sort of thing 'Post Modernist'. The clean lines and square formality of Gibberd's classic Modern Architecture are here replaced by a relaxed 'let it all hang out' approach. Humour is injected by the catering outlets, which include Petits Fours, the Four To The Bar piano lounge, and T4 Two.

When British Airways moved their long-haul operation into Terminal 4, they created a partial vacuum in Terminal 3. Half of that terminal's through-put vanished overnight. However, with passenger numbers increasing among the remaining users, it seemed clear that the vacuum would not last for ever. The BAA decided to use the respite to refurbish Terminal 3, and to increase the size of both arrival and departure buildings. The four-year £68,500,000 refit was planned to introduce more natural light into public areas, and to improve circulation by fitting new stairs, lifts and escalators. The main departures hall was extended to the south-east, to increase its area by 30 per cent. As usual by now, the alterations were carefully phased, with most work being done in the relative quiet of winter.

About a hundred yards from the airport's northern perimeter, on the other side of the Colnbrook bypass, lies the former home of The Road Research Laboratory, now hiding behind a rather anonymous sign: 'Government Building, Harmondsworth'. With the Road Lab now transferred to the wilds of Hampshire, part of this site is now occupied by the slightly sinister Immigration Detention Centre, which imprisons people who have flown into the United Kingdom and have not been able to satisfy immigration officers that they should be allowed to stay. The Detention Centre is adorned with floodlights and barbed wire. In 1986 the number of arriving foreigners whose admittance was pending further enquiries grew to an unseemly level. Many had to be kept overnight in some of the many hotels around Heathrow, with guards posted outside their rooms. The Government announced that compulsory visas would soon be introduced for people coming from India, Pakistan and West Africa, so that the immigration procedure could be sorted out decorously by the British consulates in the countries of departure. This announcement produced an even bigger rush from the countries affected, presumably consisting in large part of would-be immigrants bringing their plans forward to beat the new regulations.

Shortly after seven o'clock on Thursday morning 17 April 1986, a taxi brought to the airport Nezar Hindawi and his girlfriend. Hindawi was a tall Jordanian aged thirty-five, his hair already greying at the sides. He wore a brown suit and he had with him a cream coat and a holdall containing clothes. Concealed in a false lining at the bottom of the holdall were 3lbs of plastic explosives, and a timing device.

His companion was thirty-two-year-old Ann Murphy, an Irish chambermaid who had just started maternity leave from her job at the Hilton Hotel in Park Lane. She had met Hindawi a year before, and had been carrying his child for five or six months. He promised to marry her soon. Now she looked forward to their holiday in Palestine, due to start in just a few hours' time.

Their taxi emerged from the tunnel, sped into the Central Area, and climbed the ramp to Terminal 1 Departures. Inside the terminal building the couple talked on the land side, Hindawi saying that he would not after all be travelling with his girlfriend. As an Arab, he was prevented by his conscience from flying with El Al. He would take a later flight on another airline and join her in Palestine. In the meantime, to save time and trouble, could she please take his bag?

Ann Murphy sat alone in the departure lounge and looked inside the holdall. All she could see were clothes. Her holiday flight, number LY016 to Tel Aviv, was due to leave at 9.50 a.m.

Shortly after nine, she made her way along Pier 3, following the signs to Gate 23.

As the state airline of Israel, El Al makes a tempting target for Arab extremists, and as a consequence its security checks are the most thorough in the world. Before boarding, passengers are interrogated and frisked, the contents of their baggage examined. Sometimes these rigorous procedures delay departures for several hours. While questioning Ann Murphy, El Al staff became suspicious, and they examined her bag with particular care. They detected the false bottom in the holdall, and the police immediately converged on Miss Murphy. When the explosives were discovered she was rushed to the heavily fortified Paddington Green police station in Edgware Road, where anti-terrorist police were soon convinced of the woman's innocence. It seems that Hindawi had manipulated her emotions so that eventually he was able to use her, and their unborn child, as a human time-bomb. The powerful Syrian military explosives that she carried were programmed to explode after take-off, as the 747 flew over Europe, possibly over London itself. The Jumbo would probably have crashed, killing many on the ground as well as the 380 on board.

After the discovery, roads and airlines were watched and Hindawi's description was circulated, but he was not traced until the police received a call from the London Visitors Hotel in Holland Road, where the bomber had booked himself in. He offered no resistance to his arrest.

The bomb plot highlighted once again the vulnerability of Heathrow, and to many observers the future of the airport appeared increasingly violent. Hindawi's explosives were only discovered because he had chosen El Al as his target. Heathrow routes with security almost as tight as that of the Israelis were those of Air India, British Airways to Tel Aviv, and all flights to Belfast. Other routes appeared to offer inadequate protection. The situation concentrated the minds of the BAA and the Government, and security was tightened. Amongst measures increasingly employed were X-rays and explosives 'sniffer' devices, both previously used only on a small random selection of checked-in baggage. All hand baggage was physically searched. Clearly some compromises remained necessary, in order to strike an acceptable balance between security on the one hand, and the need to keep a busy airport running smoothly and inexpensively on the other.

Some question remains about the desirability of leaving the Central Area and Terminal 4 open to the general public. It might be safer to exclude at least from the actual terminal buildings all but those holding tickets (with special arrangements for the walk-on shuttles). Such a ban would be expensive, not only because of the personnel needed to enforce it, but also because the BAA would lose revenue from weepers and greeters using shops and restaurants.

With Margaret Thatcher's Conservative Government committed to the widespread privatization of nationalized industry, eventually it was the turn of the British Airports Authority to be sold to the public. British Telecom, British Gas and British Airways had already been successfully launched on the Stock Market. Norman Payne accepted that the Authority should be sold off in the same way, his only concern being that the group should not be split up and sold off in separate pieces. Some Tories argued that the group's airports would become more efficient in competition with each other, but finally the view prevailed that , since the BAA was consistently making profits, it was best left as one body. Airports are geographically fixed and cannot compete in the normal business sense. Besides, the desire for airlines to maximize passenger loads through interlining means that the airport which starts with the most flights starts with an unassailable advantage. The Government did see a need, however, to encourage 'financial transparency' and inhibit cross subsidy, as from Heathrow to profit-starved Prestwick. To this end, each of the seven BAA airports was made a separate company, each of them wholly owned by the same holding company, BAAplc. The change took place in August 1986, with BAAplc owned by the Secretary of State for Transport until privatization in 1987.

During the 1980s the telephone service of the Post Office became 'British Telecom', the regional gas boards became 'British Gas', and the National Coal Board was restyled 'British Coal'. Similarly, in the run-up to privatization, BAAplc dispensed with the world 'Authority', identifying itself as simply 'British Airports'.

To interest the public, most of whom had never heard of BAA, a series of advertisements appeared on British television in the spring of 1987. Brilliantly concise, the adverts concentrated on Heathrow and in the space of a few seconds managed to convey the scale of the changes at the airport. Actor Roy Marsden, in the role of a struggling post-war airline owner, was whisked by the magic of television from the humble tented terminal of 1946 to the contemporary vastness of Terminal 4.

In May the Prime Minister called a General Election for 11 June, and the BAA flotation was postponed pending the outcome of the poll.

The Tories were returned with a large majority, and in July, against the background of an enticingly bullish Stock Market, the BAA launch went ahead. To achieve their twin aims of wider share ownership and maximum profit from the sale, the Government were persuaded to try a novel dual structure with this offer. To maximize revenues from the big institutions, 365 million shares were offered for tender and sold to the highest bidders. To maximize the number of small shareholders, the remaining 260 million shares were offered to individuals at the give-away fixed price of 245p, payable in two instalments over ten months, the first instalment being 100p. On the Stock Market these partly-paid shares immediately rose to 150p, providing small shareholders with an instant 50 per cent profit.

Stories began to appear in the press about air traffic controllers working in conditions of stress and fatigue. The main ATC computer for the skies over England and Wales, situated two miles north of Heathrow at West Drayton, was rumoured to be unsuitable or inadequate, even prone to breaking down on occasion, leaving radar screens blank. There were numerous leaked reports of 'airmisses' (near misses between airborne aircraft). These came to a head with the prominent media coverage given to a close shave 18,000 feet over Lydd on the Kent coast in February 1988. A British Airways TriStar heading for Heathrow came close to hitting a Bulgarian Tu 154 bound for Gatwick. Aircraft are supposed to remain separated by at least 1,000 feet vertically and three miles horizontally. Some passengers in the TriStar later claimed to have missed the Bulgarian by a matter of feet.

It was against this background that the controllers' union complained that Keith Mack, head of the National Air Traffic Service (NATS), was planning to get rid of 135 controllers' jobs. NATS is a joint CAA and Ministry of Defence outfit responsible for preventing collisions above the United Kingdom. A Monopolies Commission report had claimed to have found unacceptable overmanning in NATS during quiet periods, when there were as many staff as during busy peaks. The controllers called instead for more staff, to alleviate increasing danger in the skies.

The CAA played down the danger. Computer failures at West Drayton had posed no threat to air safety, they assured the public. A new computer would be ready in 1990. It took ten years to clock up as many deaths through air accidents throughout the world as were recorded in just one year through road accidents in Britain alone. They pointed out that there has never been a collision between airliners over this country. Despite an explosion in the number of aircraft movements, the number of airmisses was actually falling.

The controllers' union countered that airmiss figures were worse then they appeared. Only airmisses reported by pilots became part of the official figures. Those spotted by controllers on their radar screens were not included, and the number of such occurrences was growing dramatically.

Some commentators suspected the controllers of using air traffic scare stories to protect their own work practices as much as the lives of the public. In March the CAA announced that they would henceforth publish details of all airmisses in British airspace, in an attempt to allay the growing public concern about safety. The facts were deemed preferable to wild rumour.

As a result of the new openness policy, a rash of alarming airmiss reports appeared in the media at a rate of one every few days.

A particularly narrow escape came on 15 April 1988, when two aeroplanes approaching Heathrow missed each other by 'less than a hundred yards' over Watford. The Manx Airlines BAe 146 and Cyprus Airways A310 were both following ATC instructions when suddenly the Cyprus captain saw the other plane in front of him. He immediately dived and passed beneath the Manx jet. If the incident had occurred in cloud, that avoiding action would not have been taken.

A couple of months later Concorde was reported to have had a narrow escape when it nearly hit a TriStar after take-off. In fact the two planes never came closer than two miles and, although the three-mile separation was breached, there was little real danger. Such cases made up the majority of airmiss stories. A few days later a helicopter carrying Princess Margaret was said to have come close to hitting a British Airways Jumbo near Heathrow. It turned out that the royal chopper had never come closer than 900 feet vertically, not a dangerous infringement of the 1,000 feet minimum.

More controversy lay in store for the Civil Aviation Authority. On Friday 1 July 1988 there was what amounted to a partial collapse of air traffic control over Europe. Telephone lines between the main centres were jammed as aircraft waited on the ground and circled in the air, unable to move through airways choked with traffic. Some flights were held up for hours. Many passengers had already boarded their aircraft when they were told there would be a delay until a take-off slot could be found.

This sorry state continued over that weekend, and was repeated later in the summer. The causes were numerous.

The delays always occurred around weekends, when there are always extra movements creating peaks. These are worst in the summer holiday season.

Besides peaks, traffic generally was up. The number of flights out of Britain had gone up 15 per cent in a year. Increasing personal wealth and partial fare deregulation contributed to unexpected growth.

Industrial action was often the direct cause of air chaos. Controllers in several southern European countries chose the summer for maximum disruptive effect.

The knock-on effect of such action rapidly spread the damage, with aircraft stranded in the wrong place. For example a 757 grounded in Athens could not return to Heathrow to perform its subsequent run to Copenhagen. A crew stuck in, say, Palma, were in the wrong place to man the morning flight to Stockholm. A pilot who had used his permitted duty hours by waiting to take off could not be asked to work late to get the plane back to base for the night.

One of the many causes of delay was reasssuring: safety standards were not compromised. Despite angry scenes in airport lounges and a vociferous press, no attempt was made to push up more flying aluminium than the air could safely hold.

Another reason was the lack of money and political support for

Eurocontrol, an organization which aims to combine safety with lack of delays in the skies of member states, which are to date Britain, France, Germany, Ireland, Portugal and the Benelux countries. Every government thinks it's already paying more than its fair share towards the organization. Nations are reluctant to surrender sovereignty over their own airspace. As a result traffic is handed over at national boundaries. If the airways of the receiving country are already full, then sometimes aeroplanes actually have to circle at the border. Finding out whether a clear path through Europe is available often involves telephoning the control centre in the neighbouring country. They then have to check with their neighbour, and so it goes on. Thousands of such telephone calls are made on a busy day. Apparently Europe needs more international air traffic control, free of internal boundaries and speeded up by one integrated computer system. Perhaps the carriers themselves should pay more for such a service.

Transport Secretary Paul Channon and the CAA Chairman each came under fire as the delays continued through the summer of 1988. CAA Chairman Christopher Tugendhat seemed to blame the Government's deregulation policy and the irresponsibility of charter carriers. The charter people were in a fiercely competitive business and they often planned without sufficient spare capacity to cope when something went wrong.

'British Airways have seemed to cope with a difficult situation well', observed Mr Tugendhat. 'Others seem to base their planning on the hope that everything is going to be tickety-boo from London to Lesbos, from April to October. Experience has shown us that it is rarely like that.'

Heathrow, with no charters, fared better than most during the snarl-ups. Most ATC delays were on routes south to the sun, where traffic was busiest and the industrial action most disruptive. These holiday routes are mainly served by charters, so the scheduled airlines at Heathrow had few services delayed. Flights to America were completely unaffected. Long-haul flights which normally overflew Europe could be re-routed around the congestion. While departures from Gatwick or Luton left up to forty-eight hours late, few passengers flying from Heathrow were delayed more than one hour.

# 8
# The Future

The Heathrow of the future will be partly shaped by Government policy. In June 1985 the Conservative administration published the key White Paper 'Airports Policy'.

This document recognizes the useful contribution to the British economy made by what is one of the world's greatest transport hubs. It endorses the view of Inspector of Airport Enquiries Graham Eyre that everything should be done to maintain Heathrow's lead in global aviation. The White Paper acknowledges the problems of the smallness of the site at Heathrow, the problems of noise, and the difficulty of forecasting future demand.

To understand the Government's plans for Heathrow it's helpful to look first at their policy concerning Britain's other airports, all spelt out in the 'Airports Policy' document.

At Gatwick the Government still refuses to consider a second runway. The capacity of the existing runway, about twenty-five million passengers a year, is now matched by the capacity of the terminals, since the North Terminal opened in 1988. Unless the Government experiences an extremely unlikely change of heart about a second runway, the future expansion of Gatwick is not possible.

Stansted will be London's third big airport. At present the Essex field can handle only two million passengers a year, but construction of more terminal space is under way to boost this to seven million. It will be exciting to watch the expansion here over the next couple of decades, although it will be restricted to one runway, ultimately limiting the capacity of the airport to twenty-five million, as at Gatwick. The Government told the BAA to dispose of the land which it had been safeguarding for a second runway.

Business jets are being gradually squeezed out of Heathrow and Gatwick, to be concentrated in smaller airfields in the Home Counties. Business traffic consists of both air taxis and aircraft owned by companies for moving their own personnel. The planes involved are usually small, and they have to take second place at busy times behind scheduled airliners. The Government have rejected the idea of using Heathrow's third runway for these aircraft, saying that would be too dangerous. They reject too the idea of building a special short runway for this traffic at Gatwick, this time citing air traffic control and environmental reasons. Nevertheless an explosion in the number of business aircraft is expected. Among the Home Counties airfields which will handle the growth are Luton, Biggin Hill, Hatfield, Leavesden and Southend. The Ministry of Defence is to provide business facilities at Farnborough, and even Northolt is open to civilian traffic once again, to help serve these economically vital business jets.

Government policy is to maintain Prestwick as the sole long-haul gateway to Scotland for the time being, despite its financial losses and its remoteness from population centres. All trans-atlantic flights to Scotland are still forced to use this airport. The Government recognizes the economic case for direct long-haul services to Edinburgh and Glasgow, but refuses to allow them because of noise. So Prestwick staggers on, though its role will be reviewed if its troubled finances do not improve.

The future looks rosier for Manchester, now the nation's busiest airport behind Heathrow and Gatwick. Northern MPs constantly complain that Manchester's potential is undermined by southern interests. The Government and British Airways say they have taken note, and they insist they're committed to expanding this 'regional hub', promising more foreign destinations, a second terminal, and possibly a rail link.

At Heathrow itself, British Airways are asking for a fifth terminal. It would be built on Perry Oaks, the only piece of land left which is both close to the runways and not already built on.

The reason this ideal site has not had a terminal put on it before is that it is occupied by one of the largest sewage works in Britain. Effluent from a large area of Middlesex arrives here via Mogden Works near Hounslow, where the preliminary treatment is done. At Perry Oaks the sludge is thickened up from 2.2 per cent solids to a concentration of 10 or 12 per cent, known in the trade as 'blancmange'. The removal of the 200 acres of lagoons would present formidable problems to the contractors of a fifth terminal.

Will a fifth terminal be needed at Heathrow? Will not Stansted be able to handle the growth in London for the foreseeable future? Perhaps future growth should be diverted to Manchester, to alleviate unemployment by stimulating the economy of the north of England. The various considerations seem endless.

On a purely technical level, can any more planes get in and out of Heathrow, and if so can enough be squeezed through to justify another terminal? The runways at Heathrow are already operating at capacity for much of the day. Spreading the traffic to off-peak times could allow in more planes, and boost passenger through-put, but by its nature this course of action would mean introducing timetables inconvenient to passengers. A strong argument in favour of Terminal 5 is presented by the development of airliners over the years. Their consistent increases in size have brought more and more people to the terminals at Heathrow, and many would argue that the trend is likely to continue. Recent bigger versions of the 747 support this view. But there is a contrary trend towards small aircraft for minor domestic routes,

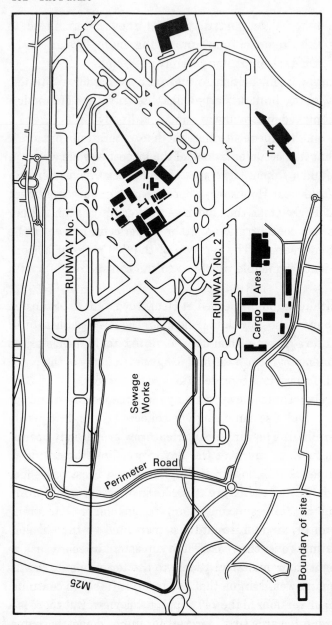

RUNWAY No. 1

RUNWAY No. 2

T4

Cargo Area

Sewage Works

Perimeter Road

M25

☐ Boundary of site

The possible Terminal 5 site

exemplified by the British Aerospace Advanced TurboProp, and Government regulation of Heathrow traffic could result in runway capacity being swamped by these smaller airliners.

Will the number of passengers wanting to use London continue to rise, or will the brakes be applied by some future economic, social or technical development?

Faced with all the uncertainties, the Government are keeping their options open on Terminal 5, placing the matter under constant review. They have asked for an enquiry into the feasability of moving the sewage works away from the airport. They have instructed the BAA to look into the possibility of modifying the existing terminals to press through another four million people a year, boosting total capacity to forty-two million.

If a fifth terminal is built, it could be enormous. British Airways would like it to be big enough to handle all their flights, which would make the terminal on its own rank as the third busiest airport in the UK. If the sewage works can be moved elsewhere, Perry Oaks could accommodate such a grand complex because the site could be extended westwards, beyond the perimeter and back a full mile, to the M25.

When London Transport extended the Piccadilly Line to serve Terminal 4, they built the loop line further west than it apparently needed to go. So far west, in fact, that it almost passes beneath the sewage works, making possible the later insertion of a tube station here to serve a fifth terminal.

Part of the appeal of BAA shares lies in the fat profits being gleaned from duty-free shops. By the year 1985/86 revenue from leases of commercial premises at the airport had grown to 50 per cent of Heathrow's income. While the air operations side lost a few millions, the commercial premises lettings made a huge £111,000,000 profit. Most of this came from duty-free sales in departure lounges. The majority of these outlets are operated by the Allders retail chain, part of Hanson Trust. Allders plan to increase turnover by positioning tobacco and alcohol at the rear of their floor space, forcing customers to pass tempting displays of expensive watches, cameras and electronics.

There are reasonable arguments against continuing to allow travellers to buy goods free of duty. Countries around the world allow small quantities of alcohol and tobacco to be imported free of tax, although the origins of the practice have largely been forgotten. In the days of sail, when voyages lasted weeks, goods were sold for the use of passengers on the journey. Since it was unreasonable to expect passengers to finish the bottle exactly on the day when they arrived at their destination, they were allowed to bring in a small amount. Now that air travel has shrunk most journeys to a few hours, duty-free concessions have lost their purpose.

The duty which is lost to governments means that in effect there is a subsidy going to air travellers, a section of the population not notably poor or deserving. The cost of hauling all those millions of bottles of alcohol around the globe amounts to millions of gallons of aviation fuel. There is also a safety argument against passenger cabins containing bottles of spirits. It will be interesting to see how long this nonsensical business continues. Already the EEC has taken steps to halt the concessions within Europe from 1992.

Since the 1940s, British Rail have had plans to link Heathrow to their national network. The favoured scheme always used to be one connecting the airport to the Feltham line, which passes to the south of the airport and runs into the central London termini of Waterloo and Victoria.

In 1988 Minister of Transport Paul Chanon announced approval for a new scheme to connect Heathrow to the Paddington line, which passes a couple of miles north of the airport. New track will be laid from the existing line due south over the M4 and into a deep tunnel beneath the airfield, to a new subterranean station serving the three older terminals. A single track will continue to Terminal 4. The 'Heathrow Express' will run, we are promised, every fifteen minutes from 5 a.m. to 11.30 at night. The electrified trains will travel at up to 100 m.p.h., covering the seventeen miles from Central Area to Paddington in seventeen minutes non-stop. Single fare about £4.

The British Rail rolling stock will be spacious, with separate First and Second classes, but it will not be taking passengers to the most handy of places. Paddington barely qualifies as central London. The new line will certainly shrink some journeys – the City will be twenty minutes closer – but passengers heading for the West End may find it quicker to stick with the tube. That will also be less hassle, with no need to change trains. It remains to be seen how many people will bother to travel out to Paddington to take the British Rail service when it starts around 1993. Clearly BAA think there will be plenty, since they are putting up 80 per cent of the £190,000,000 capital cost. The remaining cautious 20 per cent will come from British Rail.

Roads around the airport may be in for some changes. The nation's premier motorway, the M25, has been congested at peak times almost from the day it opened. The M4 at Heathrow has for many years been the busiest stretch of motorway in Britain. If the situation is to be alleviated there will clearly have to be more road capacity. The existing roads could be widened, although both the M25 and the M4 are already eight lanes wide as they approach the airport. Alternatively, we could see more motorways of the standard width, possibly running alongside the existing ones. It could even be that lack of space will necessitate noisy and ugly double-decked motorways.

The major factor shaping Heathrow in the past has always been the design of aircraft, and by far the most important aspect of their design has been size. Gradual growth from Lancastrian and Dakota to 747 and Airbus has lengthened piers, enlarged baggage carousels, and wrung an enormous passenger capacity from three runways. Big aeroplanes have brought down the cost of travel, boosting both the number of passengers and the scale of building at the airport. When Boeing were designing the 747 they considered making it a giant double-decker. Seeing the first 747 land in 1970, Peter Masefield told the press:

'This is nothing. Soon there will be aircraft big enough to make the 747 look as small as the 707.'

And aircraft will continue to get quieter. The residents of Richmond and Hounslow can look forward to a steady reduction in peak noise levels, with new generations of planes sounding ever less like Titan rockets and ever more like harmless hair-dryers. Public attitudes towards the airport will doubtless improve as a result. British Airports will try to use quieter aeroplanes as an excuse for having flights around the clock.

The propeller is about to make a sensational comeback, but with the familiar long thin blades replaced by two contra-rotating sets of short stubby blades, shaped like scimitars and mounted at the back of the engine. Boeing's 150-seater 7J7 – their rival to the Airbus A320 – is expected to take to the air in the early 1990s, pushed along by two such engines mounted at the back of the fuselage. The new propellers are being developed by all three principal engine makers, though each has given its particular version a different name – either Propfan, Ultra Bypass or Unducted Fan. All are powered by the usual jet turbine, and all can be likened to turbofans with the casing around the fan removed. It's thought they will be quieter, cleaner and up to 40 per cent more fuel efficient than the jets at Heathrow today, though Pratt & Whitney, General Electric and Rolls-Royce all have to overcome problems of safety, cabin noise and airframe vibration fatigue before the new propellers are seen at Heathrow or any other airport.

There has always been a trend towards faster and faster aero-planes, although up to now the speed of sound has held most airliners below 600 m.p.h. The tremendous energy, strength and financial commitment needed to get through the sound barrier have excluded all but Concorde and its Russian counterpart. Neither plane has been very successful, looking with hindsight like false starts in the race for mass supersonic travel.

The majority of aircraft using Heathrow now seem likely to remain subsonic until well into the next century. On a short-haul flight of a few hours there is little point in going supersonic. But for those with the money who want to cover mileages approaching five figures, a couple of plane makers are known to have extremely ambitious schemes.

British Aerospace plan a passenger version of their HOTOL spaceplane project, which would travel from Heathrow to Australia in under two hours! HOTOL stands for HOrizontal Take Off and Landing. To save undercarriage weight, the spaceplane's 334 m.p.h. take-off would be from a trolley which would be left travelling down the runway. After two minutes the plane would pass the speed of sound, then after a mere five minutes would reach five times the speed of sound, before leaving the atmosphere and travelling through space. The rotund HOTOL would have modest delta wings at the back, and tiny canard fins near the front. A lightweight undercarriage would be lowered for its 200 m.p.h. landing.

A rival project of the American McDonnell Douglas company envisages a sort of sleek elongated flying triangle with fins at the back, the whole thing powered by methane. This machine would cruise for up to 7,000 miles around Mach 5 at 105,000 feet. With an eye to the lucrative military market, the company envisages a subsequent version reaching Mach 25 and, like HOTOL, being able to deliver hardware into Earth orbit.

The Central Area terminals could be altered to be more like Terminal 4, with a single undivided lounge instead of piers and gate lounges. Alternatively, there could be a move in a quite different direction, to a concept employed at some US fields – the mobile lounge. With this system, passengers for a given flight walk into a comfortable lounge. Just before flight departure the doors are closed, and the entire lounge is then driven to the aircraft. Mobile lounges are three or four times as wide as vehicles on public roads, and as they approach the plane the lounge compartment is pushed up to the level of the aircraft door. Clearly this system requires the least physical effort from passengers, who may be conveyed thus to aircraft in quite remote and hitherto unusable corners of the airfield.

Closely related to the mobile lounge is the as yet untried 'passenger container'. Some sort of giant crane would remove from container aircraft entire sections of cabin with arriving passengers still in their seats. The arriving containers would be quickly replaced by containers of departing passengers already in their seats. This odd idea seems sensible because of the apparent saving of time at turn-round. However, routine checks, refuelling and unforeseen snags would still demand many minutes, so the cost of introducing passenger containers would seem to be offest by few benefits.

Will runways become obsolete? The business of rushing along the ground to get airborne is actually quite crude, and it may be that in the future we shall look back at this procedure with amusement. The military Harrier jet already lands and takes off vertically, and perhaps one day this space-saving technique will be applied to big passenger transports.

A new airport is being developed in the Royal Albert Dock, only five miles from the City. The cramped City of London Airport site is practicable because it caters for STOL aircraft, that is aircraft capable of Short Take-Off and Landing. So far the only aircraft with STOL capability are small and have a short range. But the ability to fly from a site near the centre of the metropolis is a valuable one, and it may become possible for large transatlantic aeroplanes to do this. The existence of Heathrow Airport might then be threatened. How long would King's Cross railway station have survived if that too were sixteen miles from central London?

In the larger perspective of history the demise of Heathrow actually seems probable. The equestrian transport hub of seventeenth-century Hounslow once handled thousands of coaches a day, yet now the stables are gone. Inland waterways were once the epitome of modern bulk transport, yet today the canals that aren't overgrown cater for little more than ramblers and anglers. Then the railways conquered the topography of Britain, and they seemed invincible. Now that network is contracting, largely superseded by motorways and airways.

If, in its turn, Heathrow does become obsolete, then will its acres become suburban streets like much of its surroundings today? Will the industries and hotels to which it has given birth be able to survive on their own, maintaining Heathrow as a commercial centre? Will society shift priorities, rediscover the value of Heathrow soil, and return the airfield to market gardens and orchards? Will the vast runways become an historic monument, the terminals a tourist attraction, and the hangars vast museums?

As the years pass into centuries is it possible that some future civilization will excavate the runways and puzzle over their purpose, just as archaeologists today ponder the meaning of Stonehenge?

# Departure

The Captain and his co-pilot, or first officer, meet in the Queen's Building an hour before their flight is due to leave. They are probably both men, as the number of women pilots remains small. If they work for a big airline with many staff, they may not have met before.

They spend about fifteen minutes gathering and discussing data in the Flight Crew Briefing Area. They interrogate computer keyboards about the technical state of the aircraft, and the weather along the route. They take a particular interest in conditions at their destination, and at airfields along the way which may have to be visited in case of emergency.

Besides conditions on the ground, there is much information about the weather at other altitudes which has to be grasped. The 100 m.p.h. winds which commonly blow at cruising height can have an enormous bearing on journey times and chosen routes.

While passengers check-in or browse in the duty-free shops, their captain and first officer seat themselves and discuss the wealth of information spread out on the table in front of them. By now they know the number of passengers they will be carrying, and the amount of freight. They discuss the coming flight, and consider any special features or unusual hazards, before making their way to the aircraft.

British Airways cabin crew assemble at Tristar House, on the

Northern Perimeter Road. They are taken in a bus directly to the aircraft stand.

The aircraft is surrounded by vehicles, and is being primed with various liquids for human and mechanical consumption. The fuel is pumped from subterranean pipes which run beneath the stand. This modern system of hydrant refuelling has made the fuel bowser a rare sight on aprons these days. The waste tanks beneath the aircraft toilets are emptied into a special lorry, known to airline personnel as 'the honey pot'. Incoming freight and baggage is removed, and replaced with the outgoing load. The cabin is cleaned. Galleys are stocked, duty-free supplies replenished. Engines are examined, wheels checked, and moving surfaces inspected. In winter, snow and ice may have to be removed.

In the cockpit, the crew buckle themselves in with straps which come over each shoulder as well as across the lap. They busy themselves with pre-flight checks. Instruments and controls are tested one by one in a sequence read from a list. They programme the Inertial Navigation System, the linked computers which, connected to the autopilot, will steer the plane to within a few miles of its destination. The INS uses sophisticated gyroscopes to guide the aeroplane from radio beacon to radio beacon. The crew key in their position at Heathrow. The equipment is so accurate that they feed in the map co-ordinates of the actual stand they are occupying.

The co-ordinates fed into the Inertial Navigation System by one pilot are checked by the other. If the aeroplane is big enough to have a flight engineer on board, then he checks the figures too. This is one example of the endless cross-checking that is universal on today's flight decks. In the search for ever higher safety standards, the pilots are trained to act as a team. There is no place for the hero who wants to fly by the seat of his pants in Battle of Britain style. No place, either, for the 'it's my turn now' attitude to flying an airliner. Individual machismo causes accidents. Instead, modern flight deck management is all about working in harmony. Cross-checking, concerns freely expressed, conflicting ideas listened to. The captain is unquestionably in command, but his crew must not be afraid to speak up if rules are broken, or danger suspected. Also a part of flight deck management is discussion of events after they have happened. Questions should be welcomed. It is part of the captain's role to hand down his experience.

During take-off, it is important that the crew know exactly what the weather is likely to be doing. At most airports this information is given to them by Air Traffic Controllers, but Heathrow is so busy that weather information is given on two separate radio frequencies, one for arrivals, one for departures. A pre-recorded tape loop gives the details in a continuous cycle, and periodically it is updated.

After listening to weather, the crew ask ATC for permission to start the engines, and for route clearance to their destination. Again, Heathrow is so busy that there is a special frequency just for this procedure. Route clearance is usually given, as a flight plan for a scheduled flight will have been stored in the ATC computer some days before. However, the delays of summer 1988 saw the widespread imposition of flow controls to keep planes on the ground until room could be found for them in the airways over Europe.

Assume no delays on this occasion. Together with route and start-up clearance, the pilots are given a 'squawk' number, which enables their aeroplane to be identified on radar screens. They dial the four-digit number into the 'transponder', which is set in the instrument panel between their seats. In flight, when the transponder is 'interrogated' by sophisticated secondary radar on the ground, it replies by transmitting this squawk number back to the radar head. The ATC computer recognizes the particular squawk and, next to the aircraft's blip on the radar screen, magically displays the flight's call sign and destination. Secondary radar also discloses the aeroplane's height in hundreds of feet. All this is a great improvement on the original 'primary' radar, which displayed all aircraft with just a blip, increasing the chances of a controller mistaking one anonymous blip for another. In the unlikely event of all their radios failing, the crew can dial in a special radio failure squawk, which lets controllers know why their instructions are not being acknowledged. In the case of a hijack, the crew can let controllers know of their predicament by surreptitiously dialling in the hijack squawk.

With the doors closed, the loading bridge retracted, and the chocks away, the pilots change frequency to ask for 'push back'. A special tractor, loaded with weights to give it grip, arrives and attaches itself to the nosewheel. The aircraft is then pushed, tail first, away from the pier, off the stand, and on to the taxiway. All the time a ground engineer walks alongside, and he is able to talk to the crew via a headset which he plugs into the fuselage. With the aircraft safely reversed and facing in the right direction, the ground engineer makes a final check that everything looks as it should from his vantage point. He then unplugs his headset, stands to one side, and raises his arm.

Another change of frequency, and the crew request permission to taxi. A large airliner is like a fish out of water when it is moving about on the ground. Little 737s manage to zip around with some ease, but 747s, with their long wings, have to be careful to avoid buildings and other aircraft. Strapped into their tiny cockpit above the 1st Class cabin, the crew see little of the ground they are rolling over. The twenty-one foot diameter fuselage below them makes it difficult to see the edge of the taxiway. Taxiing a Jumbo has been compared to driving a double-decker bus along a footpath, using a steering wheel three seats back on the upper deck! In the cockpit there are maps of airport taxiway layouts to help the crew find their way.

Aircraft moving on the ground are watched by controllers in the Ground Control Room at the top of the tower. They can see the plane they are talking to by looking through the glass that surrounds them. In fog they still get a clear picture, from a special short wave radar which shows aircraft on the ground. In great detail, this primary radar shows buildings, parked aircraft, road vehicles, and even the layout of the taxiways and runways. The orange dustbin-like housing of the head for this radar, perched above the Ground Control Room, is visible from all around the airport.

On the way to the runway the crew perform their before-take-off checks. Towards the end of the taxi they will be told to retune to the departures controller, who looks after aircraft approaching and using the take-off runway. The departures controller will know that he now has responsibility for the aeroplane because he has been handed its Flight Progress Strip. Indeed, throughout its journey, any airliner has a corresponding Flight Progress Strip which is handed from controller to controller. The system seems old-fashioned, but it is unambiguous and known to be reliable. At busy times the departures controller has several Flight Progress Strips stacked in front of him. Outside on the airfield there is a corresponding queue of airliners converging on the end of the runway. It is customary to let Concorde jump the queue. Every minute counts for a supersonic aeroplane whose customer appeal lies in time saved. Concorde's preferential treatment is accepted by subsonic crews, many of whom regard a chance of seeing this aeroplane as one of the bonuses of being put on the Heathrow run. Some captains use their intercom to point out the plane to their passengers.

Eventually it is the turn of our airliner. Told to 'line up and hold', the aircraft lumbers forward and swings into position at the end of the runway, coming to a halt with its nose pointing straight down the runway centre line. When the aircraft in front is safely off the ground and out of the way, the controller tells the pilots of our aircraft 'cleared for take-off', followed by the present read-out of wind direction and speed. With a strong cross-wind, the wing in the lee of the fuselage will experience less lift, requiring the captain to use his ailerons to keep the plane balanced.

The captain advises his crew: 'Stand by for take-off'. He pushes the thrust levers forward. The engines rapidly build up to a roar, their thrust countered by the wheel brakes. Still held in check, the aeroplane shakes as the frantic engines do their best to pull the wings off. The captain lifts his toes from the brake pedals. The silver bird starts to roll.

The runway most frequently used for take-offs is 27 Right. A big aeroplane charging down this runway is an impressive sight at close range. The noise of its engines attracts the attention of passers-by on the perimeter road, only 500 feet from the edge of the runway and separated from it by only a chainlink fence. In the past, drivers on this road often had their eyes on the aeroplanes rather than the road ahead of them, and there were a lot of car crashes. The BAA found that the answer – unpopular with enthusiasts – was to attach a screen to the fence at eye level for its entire length.

As the airliner accelerates by up to 5 m.p.h. every second, passengers are pressed into the backs of their seats. Through the windows they can see the white line which marks the side of the runway. Beyond that lies the concrete margin which is the original surface from the Second World War.

About 300 yards into its take-off roll, the plane passes over the site of Caesar's Camp, the Celtic settlement. Further along and off to the right is the site of the original RAF apron, which was flanked by tents and huts during Heathrow's first years as an airport. On the plane rushes, past Roy's cannon, and past the weather station where once the little RAF control tower stood. Further on there appears a series of gates in the perimeter fence, leading to the main fire station.

On the flight deck there is intense concentration. One of the pilots, usually the captain, actually controls the plane, steering it straight down the runway centre line. The other pilot, poised to take over in case of some sudden incapacitation, has his eyes glued to the instruments in front of him, ceaselessly scanning the dials or cathode ray tubes for anything out of the ordinary. If there is a flight engineer, he monitors the engines.

When something does go wrong, both reverse thrust and the wheel brakes are used to bring the plane to a halt. During the take-off roll, though, a point is reached when it is too late to stop because there is not enough runway left to slow down. The speed of the plane when this point is reached is known as 'V1'. V1 is calculated by the crew before take-off. It is the velocity after which they are committed to take-off. If anything crucial goes wrong after V1, the plane nevertheless has to go ahead with the take-off, before probably turning around and landing as quickly as possible.

On this occasion there is no emergency. The first officer calls 'V1' at perhaps 140 m.p.h. A few seconds later, at perhaps 160 m.p.h., he calls 'VR'. VR, velocity of rotation, is also worked out in advance. To rotate the aircraft, the pilot pulls the control column slowly towards him. This makes the tail dip towards the ground. The aircraft pivots on its undercarriage, and the nose goes up. The crew no longer see the runway ahead of them – the windscreen is now filled with sky. The aeroplane points up at an angle of 15°. The wings have some flap extended, though not the full amount. With their angle of attack increased by 15°, they give more lift. The plane lifts off the ground.

The captain calls 'Gear up', and the first officer retracts the undercarriage. This reduces air resistance and improves aerodynamics.

As the plane climbs, Perry Oaks sewage works reveals its full magnificence to passengers on the left. Beyond that, the black strip of the other asphalt runway. Further behind is the third runway, still surfaced with concrete, but decorated with black tyre marks around the touch-down zones. To the right can be seen the Bath Road, sleepy Harmondsworth, the River Colne, and the busy M25.

Heathrow control now hand responsibility for the plane to the London Flight Information Region. London FIR controls high-flying aircraft over most of England and Wales. It is based at West Drayton, where about a hundred controllers sit in front of radar screens in a large darkened room. Most control civil air-craft, though a minority dressed in RAF uniform demonstrate the Ministry of Defence involvement. Military activity has to be coordinated with civil traffic.

Heathrow, Gatwick, Stansted and Luton all lie within an area of especially complex traffic which is called the London Terminal Manoeuvring Area, or London TMA. It is the London TMA con-trollers at West Drayton who are responsible for flights after they have left Heathrow. They are now able to give our flight initial climbing clearance, to perhaps 6,000 feet, or 'flight level six zero', to use ATC parlance.

Every airliner wants to get high, where the air is thinner and the plane can travel faster and more cheaply. To a fast plane, the air at low altitude is like thick viscous treacle which the plane struggles to push its way through. Unfortunately the desire to gain altitude often has to be frustrated by ATC. The aircraft may be told to maintain a lower altitude until room is found for it up above. The first responsibility of controllers is to keep aeroplanes well separated, and London FIR is thick with aircraft.

After take-off the throttles are eased back to reduce noise on the ground. This produces an alarming sensation in the cabin, as if the plane were falling back, but in fact it continues to climb, although less steeply, and it continues to increase airspeed. Gradually the flaps are retracted.

Planes leaving Heathrow follow one of a number of predetermined departure routes, which have been drawn up to minimize noise nuisance to population centres on the ground. Charts of these noise routeings are among the documents that will have been studied by the crew before take-off. The routes are adhered to by referring to radio beacons. The London beacon, situated in a cabbage field half a mile north of the airport, is used as a reference for some departure routes. This beacon identifies itself by broadcasting the Morse code for LON.

Below, the River Thames and Windsor come into view. The London conurbation gives way to English countryside.

After reaching 6,000 feet and maintaining that height for some minutes, our airliner is given clearance by West Drayton to climb to 20,000 feet. The crew reach forward to programme the autopilot, which is just below the windscreen. They key in 20,000 feet as their selected height, together with the desired speed and rate of climb. The INS is locked on to the next radio beacon along their route, and the pilot gives control to the autopilot. The crew are thus relieved of the tedium of routine flying, until they disengage the autopilot when they are about to land. They now adopt a more detached, managerial role. They keep an eye on the autopilot to make sure it is behaving itself, and from time to time they will key in modifications to its instructions.

At high altitude, aircraft are obliged to fly along corridors ten miles wide and thousands of feet high, known as 'airways'. With names like Green One and Red Three, airways run in straight lines between radio beacons. Aircraft beginning their journeys enter the airways from below.

Airspace above the United Kingdom is busy, with a large proportion of aircraft climbing or descending. The predominant direction of travel is north/south, with much traffic also moving north-west/south-east. The aircraft making up this traffic are largely going to British regional hubs, other Western European cities, and the Middle East. In the summer the airways are filled by charters heading south to the Mediterranean resorts.

A big constitutent of the north-west/south-east flow is trans-atlantic traffic. Airliners bound for the United States follow a course which takes them north from Heathrow, leaving UK air-space over Wales, Northern Ireland or even Scotland. Many people find this surprising, as the major US cities are all south of London. Confusion about this arises from looking at flat maps of the world. Looking at a globe, you can see immediately that the shortest way to America is to take a 'short cut' by going a bit over the top, rather than following lines of longitude all the way round. Such a short cut is known as the 'great circle' route.

The great circle phenomenon means that the United Kingdom, stuck out on the north-west of the continent, has passing through its airspace much of the traffic which daily plies its way between America and the rest of Europe.

Flying activity is not distributed evenly round the globe, and the main concentration is in the United States. There people shuttle around on a scale unknown on this side of the Atlantic. Europe nevertheless ranks as the next centre of activity behind America. With the United Kingdom on the path between the two, Heathrow finds itself at the centre of the world's airways.

# Bibliography

*Heathrow and District in Times Past*
Various authors, Countryside Publications 1979

*More about Heathrow and District in Times Past*
ed P.T. Sherwood and A.H. Cox, Countryside Publications 1983

*Heathrow Before and After the Airport*
P.T. Sherwood, Hillingdon Borough Libraries, publication imminent

*Wings Over Westminster*
Harold Balfour, Hutchinson 1973

*Critch! The Memoirs of Brigadier-General A.C. Critchley*
Hutchinson 1961

*The Victorian History of Middlesex Vol IV*
ed. R.B. Pugh, Oxford University Press 1971

*Fairey Aircraft Since 1915*
H.A. Taylor, Putnam

*A History of the World's Airlines*
R.E.G. Davies, Oxford 1964

*The Challenge of BEA*
Garry May, Wolfe 1971

*Wings Across the World*
Harold Penrose, Cassell 1980

*Aircraft Alive*
Chris McAllister, Batsford 1980

*Air Traffic Control*
Graham Duke, Ian Allan 1984

# Index